DATE DUE

DUSTIN HOFFMAN

R

DUSTIN HOFFMAN
Hollywood's Anti-Hero

Jeff Lenburg

St. Martin's Press
New York

To my loving parents,
John and Catherine Lenburg

DUSTIN HOFFMAN: HOLLYWOOD'S ANTIHERO. Copyright © 1983 by Jeff Lenburg.
All rights reserved. Printed in the United States of America. No part of this
book may be used or reproduced in any manner whatsoever without written
permission except in the case of brief quotations embodied in critical articles or
reviews. For information, address St. Martin's Press, 175 Fifth Avenue, New
York, N.Y. 10010.

Design by M. Paul

Library of Congress Cataloging in Publication Data

Lenburg, Jeff.
  Dustin Hoffman, Hollywood's anti-hero.

  1. Hoffman, Dustin, 1937–   . 2. Actors
—United States—Biography. 3. Moving-picture
actors and actresses—United States—Biography.
I. Title.
PN2287.H56L46 1983   791.43'028'0924 [B]   82-17001
ISBN 0-312-22268-8

First Edition

10 9 8 7 6 5 4 3 2 1

Contents

A section of photographs follows page 84

Acknowledgments

The formidable years of writing this biography would have been at a deep loss without the help of the following sources: Frances B. Cogan of Sarah Lawrence College; Irene Mizwinski of Viacom Enterprises; Alan Levin of CCG; Mike Lefebvre of L/C Films; Joyce Penny of the Pasadena Library; Mary Corliss of the Museum of Modern Art; Charles Champlin of the *Los Angeles Times;* Howard Taubman and Stanley Kauffmann of *The New York Times;* Army Archerd of *Daily Variety;* Santa Monica City College Library and its staff; Los Angeles High School and its staff; the Academy of Motion Pictures Arts and Science Library and its staff; *Hollywood Reporter* and its staff; *Daily Variety* and its staff; and Mike Hawks of Eddie Brandt's Saturday Matinee; and interview material featuring Bob Fosse; James Leo Herlihy; Katharine Ross; David V. Picker; John Schlesinger; Pietro Germi; and, finally, Greg Lenburg, Randy Skretvedt, Jordan Young, Dave Koenig, and Bob and Louise Mazur, the latter for the use of their typewriter in a time of extreme distress.

And, lastly, special thanks to Dustin Hoffman for his innumerable contributions to the cinema, which inspired me to write this book. Also, to Charles T. Barton for always helping me to feel confident of success, no matter what happens.

1

Birth of an Antihero

Film antiheroes are best defined as sympathetic, defenseless characters ensnared in situations that often reflect the world's complex realities. These include marriage, government, social status—the whole gamut of socially related topics.

Dustin Hoffman has perhaps the longest string of antihero credits of any modern actor in Hollywood today. He has portrayed a large variety of roles in a relatively short amount of time: the confused college virgin of Benjamin Braddock in *The Graduate;* the crippled hustler of Ratso Rizzo in *Midnight Cowboy;* the grizzled old codger of Jack Crabb in *Little Big Man;* the comic outlaw of Lenny Bruce in *Lenny;* Carl Bernstein of *All the President's Men;* and even a marathon runner in *Marathon Man.* He has played them all with the precision of a dedicated craftsman, even the most difficult persona of them all: a character close to his own, Ted Kramer, a divorced parent, in *Kramer vs. Kramer.*

What Hoffman does is create characters that audiences will understand. Some say his obsession with preparation and researching characters borders on fanaticism. He goes about it like a scientist compiling as much data on a new specimen as possible, but his antihero characters relate some small seed of his own idiosyncrasies.

Hoffman is probably one of the hardest working actors around when it comes to rehearsals on the set and to helping other actors understand their characters. He has also been characterized as a perfectionist, the archetypal difficult actor devoted to making films that reach their fullest artistic potential. Maybe that is why Dustin has been so successful for so many years, along with the fact that some equally prominent writers and directors have taken the same interest in making his productions technical masterpieces.

Dustin was the second son born to Harry and Lillian Hoffman on August 8, 1937, at Queen of Angels Hospital in Los Angeles. Legend has it that his mother named him Dustin because she was a devout movie fan of Dustin Farnum, a star of silent cowboy films. But that is simply the brainchild of some Hollywood publicist. As Lillian Hoffman once remarked in an interview: "That's just not true. I'm not old enough to remember Dustin Farnum. I just liked the name; that's why I called him Dustin."

Dustin has recalled that the life of his father was similar to that of Arthur Miller's tragic stage character, Willy Loman, since the Hoffmans were never particularly well-off during his childhood. His father was a propman at Columbia Pictures until, some years later, he decided to go into business as a furniture designer. Harry Hoffman surely influenced Dustin with the burning desire to enter show business, coming home after work with a stock of Hollywood stories to tell.

Perhaps the boy's interest grew when his brother, Ronald, was able to win a walk-on role in the Frank Capra classic *Mr. Smith Goes to Washington* (1939). Though his acting career failed to pan out, Ron then tried dancing, but again met with little success. Because of his older brother's early accomplishments, Dustin has admitted he oftentimes felt inferior. He recalls, "I was always the black sheep in the family. My brother was the brilliant one. A straight-A student." When Ronald gave up his show business ambitions, Dustin began his.

Hoffman was a slow starter as a child, however. He didn't talk until he was three and his mother recalls that Dustin rode his first scooter when he was two and a half. Yet Lillian Hoffman also says that her son was *always* "a clown right from the start." At age twelve, in seventh grade, Dustin began his acting career as the shortest boy at John Burroughs High to portray Tiny Tim in *A Christmas Carol*. His acting debut was cut short, though, when an older student coaxed him into saying at the play's end, in an impish, childlike voice, "God bless us all, goddamn it!" Dustin did—and was promptly suspended from school.

Although he liked to act, in 1952 Dustin transferred to Los Angeles High School and took up classical piano. He played piano every day once home from school, dreaming about making it some day as a professional classical pianist. Dustin was called on to play in school assemblies whenever the scheduled speakers failed to show, even though he knew only one song, "Bumble Boogie" (first popularized by Freddy Martin and later reprised in the fifties by B. Bumble and the Stingers).

Besides truly loving classical piano, Dustin was very industrious. He was a member of his high school's tennis team and also track team, where he specialized in marathon running. He sold *Daily Mirror* newspapers across the street from Rexall Drugs on Beverly Boulevard in Hollywood.

As Dustin himself once recalled, "I was the Bumble Boogie ace in the hole. At parties, the first thing I did was find the piano. I would sit on the edge of the bench, leaving room for the right girl to sit down next to me, and say, 'Boy, do you have sensitive hands.' She never did."

Growing up, Dustin was, by his own recollection, "a kid who was always too short, wore braces on his teeth, and had one of the worst cases of acne in Los Angeles." Hoffman was so conscious of his height (he's 5 feet 6 inches), in fact, that in later life he spent years in analysis trying to compensate for it.

Maybe that accounts for his being so active in high school, always trying to prove to the other students that he was capable of the extraordinary. On graduation, in 1955, Hoffman set his goals even higher, working toward a degree in music while attending Santa Monica City College. During his sophomore year, Dustin decided on taking a light academic course load with an easy-credit class as one of them. The class was on the fundamentals of acting and it made him think twice about a career in music. Still confident he could make it as a pianist, however, Hoffman left Santa Monica City College and enrolled at the Los Angeles Conservatory of Music, studying classical and jazz piano.

In early 1957, Dustin again had a change of heart because he came to realize acting was his greatest joy. Doubtless, he remembered the fun he had had, not only in junior high school but also during his acting classes at college. Acting seemed to offer him greater opportunities with which to express himself than music. Having found his career objective, Hoffman left the conservatory to join the Pasadena Playhouse, where he studied the fundamentals of acting. Dustin proved to be not only a good actor but a class ham, claiming that his shy nature and interest in girls were what led him into an acting career.

"I got into acting so I could meet girls," Hoffman once confessed. "*Pretty* girls came later. First, I wanted to start with someone with two legs, who would smile and look soft. When I took a girl out, my impulse was to kiss her, but I never would. I was King of the Never Kissing. Then, in acting class we would do scenes where we were supposed to follow our impulses. My impulse was to take a girl in my arms and kiss her. I would pick certain acting classes just because of the girls in them."

He continued to win the throbbing hearts of his young playhouse pretties (one unnoticed classmate was a young Barbra Streisand), though the names of women have remained as guarded as his private life. He also caught the attention of the playhouse directors and finally got a break: the chance to play the lawyer in the school production of *A View from the Bridge*. The play's director, Barney Brown, a very demanding type, felt Dustin had the special ingredients to play the role effectively. In fact, his actual words to Hoffman after the production closed were, "I'll tell you kid, you got something. It's going to take a long time. But you're going to make it. How long? You'll probably be thirty before anything happens."

In 1958, taking Brown's advice to heart, Dustin decided that California was not the place to be for a fledgling actor. New York was the glamour spot in which every actor found his start. And it was in the Big Apple that Hoffman would eventually wind up, so as, in his words, "not to fail at home."

2

New York, New York . . .
Off-Broadway work, *A View from the Bridge, Madigan's Millions*

Hoffman never wavered from his determination to become an actor, since what he wanted most in life was a career in show business. And work he did. Dustin continued performing in stage productions for the Pasadena Playhouse before going east to try his luck in New York. Friends were encouraging him to make the trip, even though New York had started gaining the reputation as "a vast wasteland for actors," and Dustin had to assure his parents that he was making the right decision before taking off for the Big Apple.

During his trip across the country, however, Hoffman made stops along the way in such midwestern towns as Steamboat Springs, Colorado, and in Fargo, North Dakota. There he became actively involved in community theater productions for over three months, gaining valuable experience before reaching New York, and acting in as well as directing some of America's most time-honored plays: William Gibson's *Two for the Seesaw,* Arthur Miller's *Death of a Salesman,* and William Saroyan's *The Time of Your Life.*

When Hoffman finally arrived in New York, his first step was to gain admission to a prominent acting school. The largest and most respected school was Lee Strasberg's The Actors Studio. To enter the school's program, each student had to undergo a preliminary audition before some of the studio's top directors. Hoffman was never so nervous in his life. His first audition, in his own words, was a "disaster." Keenly aware that the audition meant everything, he just couldn't relax. When he was rejected, Dustin didn't quit. He auditioned *four* more times, failing each time, and was never notified as to why he failed.

Dustin kept up his unsuccessful search for another acting school in the area, until, several months later, he was recommended—and finally accepted at—The Actor's Studio. Strasberg's classes had spawned the likes of Marlon Brando, George C. Scott, and Marilyn Monroe. The famous instructor took an instant liking to Hoffman and helped make the necessary arrangements for his enrollment in the school's program. His two roommates, Robert Duvall and Gene Hackman, also learned the fundamentals of acting from Strasberg.

In between classes, Dustin ferreted out bit parts in off-Broadway and college productions. But acting jobs were scarce, and he tried a series of short-term jobs in order to support himself, starting as psychiatric attendant in a mental hospital. Of his first day in the men's ward, Dustin remembered, "I was scared silly! Charging down the hall was a middle-aged guy. He said to me, 'I'm getting out next Sunday . . . my wife's an old Dutch cleanser . . . you got nice teeth, sonny boy, are they yours?" Rambling on senselessly, the man, without warning, suddenly started making the noise of an electric razor, unnerving Hoffman considerably.

About a month later, Hoffman decided he had had enough working with such loonies, and took on another part-time job as a typist. Dustin was very efficient, capable of pounding out eighty words a minute, but clerical jobs were far from challenging. So he would quit, usually after working a half a day on these various jobs.

At least Dustin managed to hold down the same job for three consecutive seasons. Three Christmases in a row he worked in the toy department at Macy's department store. One year his job was selling hockey games, which retailed for $16.95. In an attempt to boost sales, Dustin came to work one morning dressed in a Montreal Canadians' hockey sweat shirt and faked a French accent while demonstrating these games for customers. Whether sales increased, no one really knows. It is known that Dustin's penchant for practical jokes never ceased to surface. On another occasion, he jokingly sat Gene Hackman's eighteen-month-old son on the countertop, selling him to some woman as "a life-size doll" for sixteen dollars.

Eventually, despite the fun, Dustin outgrew his job as a toy salesman and yearned to get closer to the theater. The closest he came to acting during the next six months was as a hatchecker at the Longacre Theatre in New York. His temporary position at the theater was during the stage run of *Rhinoceros* with Zero Mostel. Hoffman has said that after he finished checking each theater patron's coat, he would sneak inside the show and focus his attention on the different actors in the play. He kept his eyes glued to the actors' given reactions in every scene—and these various styles of acting were subsequently absorbed into his own style. When *Rhinoceros* ended its stage engagement, however, Dustin took to the streets, landing a wide variety of menial jobs, including janitor at a dance studio, weaver of Hawaiian leis, and waiter. A short time later, he also taught acting at the East Harlem Boys' Club on 110th Street in New York.

Although he was short of making it on Broadway, Dustin was making definite headway in another direction: He had gained a citywide reputation as a ladies' man. As one anonymous writer recalls: "He became, in fact, something of an underground Warren Beatty." When Hoffman came to New York, something happened to his outward personality—something that made him easily acceptable to women. He attributes his success to his approach, such as reading girls Carl Sandburg and romancing them by playing the piano. As his longtime friend Robert Duvall recalls, "Dustin had more girls than anybody I've ever known—more than Joe Namath ever dreamed about." Modestly, Dustin has always downplayed his image as a womanizer.

Besides his enormous ability to romance women, Dustin also went through a period when he started growing his hair long and began changing his wardrobe to leather boots, blue jeans, and a sheepskin vest without a shirt. His favorite means of transportation, other than an automobile, was a motorcycle. Blending in with college hippies and anti-Vietnam protestors, Dustin's clothes were a sign of the times.

Yet, no matter what direction his appearance took, Dustin continued experiencing setback after setback in launching his career. The main reason: Hoffman had become unaggressive. As he once recalled, "Bob Duvall and Gene Hackman and I would put our pictures underneath the door and run rather than wait to be interviewed and get rejected. We were not salesmen. We would back into a spotlight rather than walk directly into it."

Hoffman tried correcting the problem, but his success at theater auditions kept coming up short of job offers. It just wasn't getting any easier. Dustin kept motivating himself and kept reading for Broadway, but producers kept turning him down. In the meantime, he took on a nonpaying offer to act in a Sarah Lawrence College production of Gertrude Stein's *Yes Is for a Very Young Man,* which opened May 20, 1959. In order to fill male roles, the all-girls college's theater department went outside the grounds to find young, budding actors. The role he won was small and the production was a far cry from Broadway, but at least it was work.

Although the production was a resounding success for the college, local critics weren't as enthusiastic and said that the play's story line collapsed under "the heavy burden of allusiveness Miss Stein imposes on it." The story itself concerned the bitterness and division that wrenched French families during the war in France. Since Hoffman was in such a minor role, there was no mention of his name in reviews, yet it did provide minor exposure for him. This led to his Broadway debut with a one-word walk-on as a nutty soldier in *A Cook for Mr. General.* Reviews for the show were lukewarm and it closed after only three weeks, throwing Dustin back on the unemployment line. His luck, however, soon changed.

The turning point of his career came when he joined the Theatre Company of Boston and became a character actor. He started honing his talent for sixty-five dollars a week, doing ten plays in nine months—works by Brecht, Beckett, Ionesco, Pinter, Sartre, and Eliot. His best performance, critics say, was as Pozzo the slave driver in *Waiting for Godot,* which played one night at the Circle in the Square in New York and was directed by Ulu Grosbard. Grosbard had nothing but the highest praise for Hoffman's performance, telling reporters afterward, "Until he did it [Pozzo], I never understood the role."

It was after the production closed that Hoffman be-

gan receiving offers from Broadway producers. One of
them was from Grosbard, who wanted Dustin to serve as
assistant director on *A View from the Bridge* (the same
play he starred in while attending the Pasadena Playhouse). Grosbard, along with film producer Joseph E.
Levine, was backing the show, which was adapted from
the Arthur Miller play. The production first opened on
Thursday, January 28, 1965, at the Sheridan Square Playhouse in New York and was the first revival of *Bridge* in
ten years. It was originally produced in one act, but this
time around, it was divided into two acts with an inter-
mission.

A View from the Bridge tells the story of an Italian
Brooklyn longshoreman who is consumed by his attrac-
tion to a young niece he and his wife have sheltered and
raised. The longshoreman was effectively played by Robert Duvall and received an equally strong and vivid performance from Jon Voight as the young man whom the
niece loves. (Voight was to work with Hoffman again,
much later, as the lead in *Midnight Cowboy*.)

On December 11, 1966, *A View from the Bridge* ended
its successful run after 780 performances. Dustin didn't
hang around for the entire engagement, however, since
he was auditioning for a new Broadway revue, *Harry,
Noon, and Night*, written by Ronald Ribman. Director
George Morrison recalls that audition: "Dustin's audition
was the most brilliant I've ever seen. It was incredible. He started grabbing props and improvising." Later,
when Hoffman latched onto the part, Morrison said that
he "retreated into himself in an attempt to understand
his character." One day, in fact, he disappeared in front
of Morrison's eyes and nobody was able to find him—not
even the director. The next day he emerged and returned
to rehearsals ready to light up the stage with his performance.

The production—the story of a writer whose room-mate Immanuel is homosexual—was first staged in the spring of 1965. Morrison has remarked that this adaptation of Ribman's story was smartly produced and well cast. The part Hoffman won was that of the hunchbacked German homosexual. Says Morrison: "In the end, his part was brilliantly realized. It was an incredible meeting between playwright and actor. It was like Tennessee Williams and Geraldine Page, Eugene O'Neill and Jason Robards, an actor finding his playwright and suddenly realizing his talent." Playwright Ronald Ribman added: "Dustin had the ability to annihilate his own ego and become the character he was looking for." (Such praise didn't go unnoticed; Hoffman was signed to guest star in an episode of television's "The Defenders," which was telecast on April 8, 1965.)

The longer he worked in a particular role, the more established he became as a stage actor; the less he worked, the more alienated he felt about stage work, and the steady work was helping. As Hoffman's flair for acting started showing steady improvement, Broadway and film producers began noticing his remarkable skills. Among the many interested parties was Frank D. Gilroy, who was recasting his Pulitzer Prize-winning play, *The Subject Was Roses*. Gilroy had spotted Dustin in a minor church production and was in awe over his agility on stage. Afterward, he asked Hoffman if he'd be interested in portraying Timmy Cleary, the son of John and Nettie Cleary, a role which Martin Sheen had played in the original production.

Hoffman agreed, reporting to rehearsals that same week. Cast changes were being made so that the original cast of Sheen, Jack Albertson (who was to win an Oscar for best actor in the film version), and Irene Dailey could take the production on tour to Los Angeles. Gilroy had decided that the show would play continuously until the new cast was ready. Hoffman was clearly excited over being selected as one of the lead actors, since it would mark his first *major* Broadway role.

Fate stepped in, however. Following Dustin's first day of rehearsal, he went over to his girl friend's house that evening to cook beef fondue for dinner. Somehow, the fondue pot exploded, showering him with searing cooking oil and starting a small kitchen fire, which Hoffman tried putting out with his hands. Dustin incurred third-degree burns on his hands, but he didn't go to a local hospital or physician for treatment, reluctant to jeopardize his opportunity to perform on Broadway in an award-winning show. His burns were much more severe than he realized, and a serious infection spread into his bloodstream, causing Hoffman to remain hospitalized for a month. Doctors listed his chances of survival as "touch and go." Thanks to proper medical care, the infection was cured and, afterward, Dustin was warned that in the future his health should come first.

After four weeks of recuperating, Dustin was released from the hospital. Despite his hands being still lightly wrapped with gauze, he was anxious to return to work. But when Hoffman showed up for rehearsal for the first time in a month, he learned that his understudy, Walter McGinn, had stolen the role of Timmy from him. Dustin couldn't help but cry. Gilroy came over to console Hoffman, explaining that the show was to open in several weeks and that with him in the hospital indefinitely, a choice had had to be made. Clearly sympathetic, Gilroy made Dustin an offer: He could become McGinn's understudy and assume the duties of assistant stage manager. Dustin, feeling double-crossed and hurt, refused the offer and stormed out of the theater. If everything had worked out, Hoffman would have played in *The Subject Was Roses* for at least a year. As it turned out, his association with the production lasted just one rehearsal.

Having the role of Timmy Cleary snatched out from under him was the one crushing blow Dustin wasn't expecting. His ego shattered, he contemplated giving up acting entirely and returning to college to earn a degree, becoming a teacher, or finding some other line of employment. The longer he thought about quitting, however, the more he realized he couldn't. Dustin still had that burning desire to become an actor. Quitting wasn't in his game plan.

Dustin tried to put his career back on track and went to auditions weekly. He struck gold about a month later when he was cast in *Sergeant Musgrave's Dance.* On the sixth day of rehearsal, however, the director told him to take a day off, or perhaps two days or more. What he meant was not to come back. For reasons still unclear, the director was evidently unhappy over Dustin's performance and occasional temper tantrums. These sudden outbursts were not uncommon for Hoffman, who has habitually got his way through arguments. Losing the job was another bad jolt, but Dustin wasn't about to give up.

He had heard through the grapevine that auditions were being held for another stage revue, *The Journey of the Fifth Horse,* by Ronald Ribman. But Dustin was almost fired *again,* this time because director Larry Arrick didn't think Hoffman "was giving enough of himself at rehearsals." Dustin quickly changed his attitude and gave Broadway a performance unequaled in years.

On April 21, 1966, *The Journey of the Fifth Horse* made its debut at New York's Off-Broadway American Place Theatre. The play was mostly drawn from a short story of Turgenev's, entitled "Diary of a Superfluous Man." The hero is a nineteenth-century Russian landowner named Chulkaturin who, dying young, leaves behind him a diary that tells the story of his life. On his deathbed he instructs his old maidservant to burn the diary after his death. Instead, the greedy servant tries selling the diary to a prominent book publisher. The plot of this Russian novella is woven with two new acts written by Ribman. The acts feature Hoffman as Zoditch, a crusty old publishing clerk responsible for reading the diary.

The play moves on three acts: Chulkaturin's life, as based from Turgenev's story; Zoditch's own life; and Zoditch's fantasies. Critics agreed that Hoffman was spectacular in his portrayal of the eccentric clerk. Some reviewers, however, questioned Ribman's combination of an old Russian tale with two acts of brand-new material, believing it was confusing and difficult to follow. One New York critic wrote that Ribman's version of Chulkaturin was "too much of an abruptly asocial boor, rather than a lonely man barred from love by a moat of ineptness."

As far as Hoffman's performance was concerned, *The New York Times* critic Stanley Kauffmann enthused: "Dustin Hoffman's performance of Zoditch has the vitality of the born actor and the fine control of the skillful one. With sharp comedy techniques, he makes this unattractive man both funny and pathetic. Mr. Hoffman is only in his twenties. Perhaps—the insanities of the theater world permitting—we will be allowed to watch an extraordinary career develop."

While the production received mild reviews, theater critics showed their appreciation for Hoffman's performance by awarding him off-Broadway's most coveted honor: the 1966 Obie Award for best actor.

With *The Journey of the Fifth Horse* confirmed as a

smash hit, Dustin appeared to be established as a stage character actor as well. He followed his command performance in Ribman's production with another top-notch antihero role in Henry Living's British comedy *Eh?* Masterfully directed by Alan Arkin, the comedy splashed onto the Off-Broadway stage on October 16, 1966, at the Circle in the Square. Arkin became the third director on the show prior to its opening, since two previous directors quit the production over "creative differences."

In this comedy revue, Dustin was starring in the lead role for the first time in his career. This time he was playing a goofy cockney machine operator named Valentine Brose who runs the boiler room of a semiautomated antiseptic dyeing factory, taking the job because it's easy work and nonunion. Following the premiere, critics were describing Hoffman's performance as "a cross between Ringo Starr and Buster Keaton." It was his ineptness with machinery that did him in, critics said, much the same as it had Chaplin in *Modern Times.*

In an interview, Arkin remarked that Hoffman had cornered a very difficult role and shown no signs of giving up. "There are two kinds of people who are difficult—those who are passionate about their work and those who are passionate about themselves. Dustin is passionate about his work. I found it a marvelously happy situation. I think we pulled it out of the hat," Arkin said.

The production was really a farce that included all the necessary ingredients—double takes, malapropisms, and standard gags. Fortunately, the story was so smartly written that the comedy material, though vintage, meshed well together. As Eliot Fremont-Smith, critic for *The New York Times,* enthused: "All involved deserve laurels. But because it is essentially Brose's show,

the biggest should go to Mr. Hoffman, who must be reck-
oned one of the most agile and subtly controlled comedi-
ans around. He carries the show and even if *Eh?* still
doesn't sound enticing, he should be seen."

Hoffman was seen, all right. Television and film producers converged on *Eh?*, reviewing his potential as a
screen personality. With *Eh?* his second smash hit, he
had become a hot commodity—so hot that he didn't
know what to do for an encore. Dustin was now in the
enviable position actors crave: He didn't have to rush; he
could scrutinize his next role.

What Dustin yearned for most of all was the opportunity to star in movies. That had been his ultimate goal
since he started acting, and he certainly wanted to see it
happen. And why not? He definitely had the face and
presence for movies, not to mention the acting ability. In
the meantime, however, he wondered when the chance
would ever come.

Fortunately, his dream came true sooner than he had
imagined possible. In October 1966, Dustin was released
from his role in *Eh?* to film a forty-five-second cameo as a
beatnik lover in Columbia Pictures' contemporary comedy *The Tiger Makes Out*. The film starred Eli Wallach and
Anne Jackson and was based on Murray Schisgal's prize-
winning play, *The Tiger*. Dustin didn't have to travel far
to appear in the film, since director Arthur Miller was
filming on location in New York. When the film was released to critical acclaim on September 19, 1967, Hoffman
was listed as nineteenth on the billing—a far cry from
top-billing in Broadway productions—but a start, none-
theless.

Although his appearance in the film was minor,
Dustin realized that he had to gain experience somehow
if he was going to break into film-making full time. In

fact, that second opportunity came faster than Hoffman had expected, when he was signed to star in his first feature film as a lead character, in the low-budget Italian-Spanish detective comedy *Madigan's Millions.* Filming began in April 1967 in Rome, with foreign filmmaker Stanley Prager directing. George Raft was originally set to take the lead as Madigan, but turned down the offer weeks before filming began. Good thing, too, since the film had a cheap budget to match its hapless script. Raft's replacement was the irrepressible Cesar Romero, who was cast opposite Italian starlet Elsa Martinelli. The film was one of several being produced by Group W Films, a foreign film company owned by Westinghouse.

When filming was completed, Dustin returned to New York to take his final bow in *Eh?*

3

The First Big Break
The Graduate

After finishing *Madigan's Millions*, Dustin's rigorous schedule never slowed down. He continued to perform eight shows weekly as the cockney plumber in *Eh?* Critics kept comparing him to Chaplin and Keaton, while the *Times* of London acclaimed him "the finest new American actor." The role won him the Drama Desk, Theater World, and Vernon Rice awards as well.

Eight shows per week still left plenty of opportunities for film agents and producers to drop in unexpectedly. Director Mike Nichols and producer Lawrence Turman, who were struggling with a film version of Charles Webb's novel *The Graduate*, took in the show one night. They had held up production of their comedy-drama movie to search out a young man who exactly fit their concept of the story's title character. Originally, they were looking for a blond surfer-type to fill the role; Hoffman hardly fit the bill. After watching his performance, however, Nichols and Turman believed he might have the necessary elements to make the character work.

The role was that of an innocent college graduate named Ben Braddock, who is seduced by an older
woman (Anne Bancroft). The cast call sheet depicted him
as well-fed, well-bred, and handsome—"a walking surf-
board," Hoffman later quipped. At age thirty, Hoffman
was a decade older than the character in the novel. But
Nichols gambled and hoped that Hoffman's talent would
triumph over his appearance.

When Hoffman arrived in Hollywood, he was one of
a long line of candidates tested in a ten-minute scene
with Katharine Ross. As Hoffman later recalled: "I was so
nervous and fatigued that I couldn't concentrate. I blew
lines repeatedly and did a terrible job, and I knew I
wouldn't get the part."

In the screen test, Dustin found himself sitting on a
bed and being instructed to play a love scene with Katharine Ross. As Hoffman once remembered: "I'd never
asked a girl in acting class to do a love scene before. No
girl asked me either."

Ross shared the sentiment, since her first impression
of Hoffman as a naïve college kid was quite unfavorable.
"He looked about three feet tall, so dead serious, so hu-
morless, so unkempt," Ross recalled in an interview. "I
thought the screen test was going to be a disaster."

It nearly was. At one point, Hoffman was so nervous
that he reached out and grabbed Ross's derriere. Ross advised him to kindly keep his hands to himself from then
on. Yet beneath Dustin's nervousness, Nichols found in
his performance the exact kind of confused, panicky
character he wanted. Because of Dustin's uneasiness on
the set, Nichols also recognized that he understood the
sufferings of Ben Braddock.

Nichols remembers the screen test was not nearly as
disastrous as Hoffman professes: "It didn't seem good

when we were making it. He didn't know his lines terribly well, and he was nervous. But it was good on film. It was special—he made us laugh. He had a kind of pole-axed quality with life, but great vitality underneath. On screen he appeared to be simply living his life without pretending." To Dustin's astonishment, Nichols offered him the part of Ben Braddock and paid him seventeen thousand dollars—not twenty thousand dollars as has been erroneously reported—for his performance in *The Graduate*.

When Hoffman learned he had won the role, he was elated, later remarking, "I had read the book and I didn't feel right for the role. The fellow in the book was tall, handsome, athletic. But Mike Nichols apparently wanted to cast it offbeat. Even when I was told I had won the role, I agreed to do it only because of my respect for Nichols as a director." The money Nichols offered was definitely also a factor in the decision.

During the first three weeks of filming, Dustin was unsettled and self-conscious. Gradually, with Nichols's guidance, he improved. One problem was the fact that for the first time he was playing a character close to his own: a very shy, intelligent, not very articulate boy trying to be polite, trying to be honorable, trying not to lie.

Dustin comically remembered also the time when he had to play a bedroom scene with Anne Bancroft. It was difficult for him, not because it meant being in bed with Bancroft, but because the crew was watching. To overcome his nervousness and shyness, he pretended that he was another man trying to bed Bancroft while all of the crew members gawked at him.

In *The Graduate*, Dustin becomes one with the character of Benjamin Braddock, who has just returned from college. His scholastic career has been nothing short of spectacular—he's not only the senior editor of the school paper but also a track star—yet he's depressed and undecided about his future. Ben's confusion about his career is further aggravated at a homecoming party given for him by his parents, at which a hoard of his father's associates pressure him to reap the rewards of the corporate life. Pressure of a different kind is also applied by Mrs. Robinson (Anne Bancroft), who finds Ben attractive. Disregarding the fact that she's married to the partner of Ben's father, Mrs. Robinson exploits Ben's politeness by getting him to drive her home. Ben attempts to leave quickly, but Mrs. Robinson again snares him and almost traps him into a seduction.

The sexual escapades are quickly terminated when Mr. Robinson unexpectedly arrives home, but Ben eventually decides that he's intrigued. He arranges a romantic liaison at a posh hotel, and despite his rather clumsy efforts at seduction, Ben engages in a clandestine affair with Mrs. Robinson—until he is smitten by her daughter, Elaine. Ben's parents, worried about their son's listless condition, arrange a date between him and Elaine, and Ben tries to discourage romance by acting boorishly and taking her out to a strip joint. But the evening ends with Ben deciding to win her.

In an effort to start their relationship out right, Ben tells Elaine about his affair with her mother, but his honesty results with Elaine hastily departing for Berkeley, where her studies and a marriage of convenience to an Ivy Leaguer await. Ben, finally spurred into action, pursues her to Berkeley—and all the way to the altar. He arrives just as the wedding ceremony is being completed, but his impassioned cries for Elaine make her forget her vow of a few moments earlier, and she rushes to join Ben. The couple flees the irate and confused members of the wedding party, taking refuge on a city bus. After a brief moment of bliss, they depart for an unknown destination—with Ben beginning to wonder about his future, as Simon and Garfunkel's title song of "Mrs. Robinson" plays.

The Graduate was Mike Nichols's second directorial effort, and Hoffman's second starring role in a film (although it might well be argued that this was his first film appearance of any stature). Nichols's style comes off as youthful, with a show-offy exuberance. He sometimes strives for unnecessarily artsy effects (such as the Eisenstein-influenced moment when Ben, having just been trapped by Mrs. Robinson, whirls around in three close-ups to face his captor), but fortunately most of the splashy techniques do help convey the inner thoughts of the characters.

Hoffman, meanwhile, demonstrates his knowledge of the comic vocabulary throughout the film. His performance is crucial to the film, because despite the witty dialogue, there is nothing inherently funny in the plot or situations. Thanks to the skill of Hoffman and the supporting players, what might easily have been a sordid, tasteless story turned into a sparklingly funny romp.

The Graduate also marked Dustin's first test on screen in a major antihero role. His character of Benjamin Braddock was an antihero in the sense that he wasn't out to glorify his successes, despite his parents' pressure. As well, his confusion with his life and a professional career swept him into situations that further compounded any kind of heroism on his part. His winning Elaine back cannot be perceived as Hollywood's typical hero-to-the-rescue scene but, rather, as an act of confused love. Even though he materially got back what he wanted, in snatching Elaine, he wasn't sure why. In the final analysis,

Dustin certainly got mileage out of taking Benjamin Brad-dock's character to the borders of serious drama and comedy, again showing his versatility as an actor.

Consequently, *The Graduate* was a gigantic box-office smash for Embassy Pictures, the film's producing company. Film revenues soared to $30 million seven months after its theatrical release, surpassing the previous domestic box-office leader of Walt Disney's, *Mary Poppins*. The film was also greeted by near-unanimous critical praise upon its public release in December 1967. *Time* touted Hoffman as "a symbol of youth" who represented "a new breed of actors." *Newsweek* likewise acclaimed Hoffman for his work and commended director Mike Nichols for presenting "an unforgettable portrait of a boy caught in the full panic of self-discovery and dragged screaming into manhood." *The New York Times* critic Bosley Crowther also tossed in his bouquet of critical kudos for Hoffman, saying that his portrayal of Ben Braddock was "believable and sympathetic."

Critics weren't the only ones who made public their opinions of the movie. Newspapers across the country were deluged with thousands of letters from fans expressing their favorable and unfavorable views of the film. A letter from a Stony Brook University student in New York, published by *The New York Times*, read: "I identified with Ben . . . I thought of him as a spiritual brother. He was confused about his future and about his place in the world, as I am. It's a film one digs, rather than understands intellectually."

In his monthly column for *Ladies' Home Journal*, veteran NBC news commentator David Brinkley sharply disagreed with critics supporting *The Graduate*. As he wrote: "Young people love this movie . . . because it puts down parents as immoral clods. It was far from the best movie I ever saw, and except for a few minutes at the beginning,

I thought it was pretty bad. It seems to me *The Graduate* only makes a few exaggerated points about familiar facets of life and then slides off into the kind of frantic non-sense Mack Sennett would have made if he had the money."

Brinkley was a member of but a small legion of crit-ics, media-oriented and otherwise, who disliked *The Graduate* and Hoffman. The National Catholic Office for Motion Pictures was another, dismissing the film with an A-4 rating for Catholics ("morally objectionable for adults, with reservations"). As a spokesman for the film-rating office said in an interview at the time: "Though the film's moral statement is evident, its impact is diminished by a romantic ending which appears psychologically false in view of the sordid relationship which has preceded it. Moreover, various details in the film's treatment may im-press some as unnecessary and even offensive."

The "offensive" qualities the National Catholic Office for Motion Pictures spokesman singled out also offended another civic-minded group. Americans of Italian De-scent registered a protest with the producers of the movie over an actor's use of the word *wop* in the film.

Joseph Jordan, AID's program coordinator, re-quested that Embassy Pictures delete the word from the film. Part of the text of Jordan's letter to the studio ap-peared in *Film Daily*, a major Hollywood trade magazine. It said: "We have been besieged by telephone calls and letters from many of our members and friends who are appalled at the slur in the movie *The Graduate*, which we would like to believe was unintentional. I refer to the line spoken by one of the actors to Dustin Hoffman, 'That's a beautiful red wop job [car] you have out there,' referring to an Italian-make car, which may not be a verbatim quote but certainly does use the word *wop*."

The letter went on to ask Embassy Pictures to rectify

the situation of "uncalled-for defamation" by deleting the word from all its prints and through careful editing of future scripts that contain such dialogue. Nothing came of the group's protest, however, as the film still contains the word *wop* in that particular scene.

Although the movie left some groups in an uproar, it also provided its share of hilarious offscreen newsbreaking moments. In the wake of the tremendous publicity Hoffman was receiving from *The Graduate*, one humorous incident resulted in May 1968. Officials for the Las Vegas Sahara Hotel were surprised when a man named Dustin Hoffman registered for a one-week stay at the hotel. Believing him to be the actor, hotel officials rolled out the red carpet for Hoffman. He was given VIP treatment around the clock and was in constant demand by the media. He answered every question posed by newspaper reporters and attributed his sudden success in movies to his parents for their unwavering support throughout the years.

On Wednesday of that week, Hoffman was seen dating a mysterious woman at the opening of Dean Martin at the Sands Hotel, demanding a ringside table. But maître d' Phil Goldman, who hadn't seen *The Graduate*, turned him away. Later, hotel officials discovered that the man was an impostor. His real name was Harvey Pepper, a twenty-three-year-old native of Montreal, Canada, who looked like Hoffman. Pepper explained in an interview: "When I came to the hotel I was sort of looking for work. Then everybody said they saw *The Graduate*, and I said I was Dustin Hoffman. So I let them think it and played the game."

It proved to be a costly game, since Pepper was arrested and spent twelve hours in the Clark County jail. His sentence was terminated when Sahara officials bailed him out and said they would absorb the cost of his room, but that he would have to pick up the food and drink tab himself.

Dustin was relaxing all right, but not in Las Vegas. He had returned home to New York following the release of *The Graduate*. Like his imposter Pepper, however, Hoffman was also dating a woman of mystery, later to be identified as Anne Byrne, a dancer. Dustin reportedly met Byrne in a Laundromat.

As the torrent of critical kudos and rave reviews poured in, it was also announced that the Hollywood Foreign Press Association had awarded *The Graduate* five Golden Globe awards. Among them were best picture; best director, Mike Nichols; best actress in a musical or comedy, Anne Bancroft; most promising male newcomer, Dustin Hoffman; and most promising female newcomer, Katharine Ross.

In April 1968, the critical appreciation of *The Graduate* continued gaining momentum going into that year's Academy Awards ceremony in Hollywood. Nominated for best picture, the film was also nominated along with such prestigious films as Warner Bros.' *Bonnie and Clyde*, starring Warren Beatty; *Dr. Doolittle*, a United Artists Picture; Columbia Pictures' *Guess Who's Coming to Dinner?*; and another United Artists' entry, *In the Heat of the Night*.

When the envelopes were presented and the winners were announced, only Mike Nichols garnered an Oscar as best director for *The Graduate*. Hoffman lost to Steiger for his brilliant performance in *In the Heat of the Night*, which also took best picture. Katharine Hepburn, for her lead role in *Guess Who's Coming to Dinner?* beat out Anne Bancroft for best actress. And Katharine Ross, who was nominated for best supporting actress, was edged out by Estelle Parsons for her sterling portrayal in *Bonnie and Clyde*.

The Oscar loss was quite a letdown for Hoffman,

even though he tried not to show it. Following the gala awards presentation, Dustin said that he was grateful that he didn't win an award. He looked at it positively in the sense that he wanted to avoid a pitfall most newcomers fall into of becoming overexposed. Losing the award would serve as the necessary stopper to a brink of media blitzes and the kind of Hollywood ballyhoo that often destroys celebrities rather than establishes them. Hoffman explained his reason for not capitalizing on his success: "Get what you can. Certainly. But at the same time, shrewdness, quite apart from any kind of artistic integrity thing, tells me that I have more longevity and more respect, the straighter I play it."

For Hoffman, playing it straight was easy.

4

Things Pick Up

John and Mary, Jimmy Shine, Midnight Cowboy

The phenomenal success of *The Graduate* continued to establish Dustin's credibility and helped him earn his keep as one of Hollywood's brightest and youngest stars. Despite all the hoopla that ensued, however, Hoffman had to collect $55 a week from unemployment because he had already squandered his $17,000-salary from the film.

It marked the first time Dustin had to battle the rigors of unemployment since he had first tried finding work in New York as a stage actor, in 1958. Though it was also a question of improving his sagging bank balance, Dustin insists that even during the harshest years of his struggle he never viewed money as a driving motivation. "I never earned more than three thousand dollars a year before I was thirty-one years old. If my parents hadn't sent me money every week, I couldn't have survived," he once said. Keenly aware that his unemployment was only temporary, Dustin waited patiently for his agent to present him with some substantial movie and stage offers.

In December 1968, after reviewing a slew of film and stage offers, Hoffman's agent came through. Several had been laid on the agent's desk—one as star in a contemporary love story for Twentieth Century-Fox and another as a lead in a Broadway comedy revue, *Jimmy Shine*, written by Murray Shisgal. Dustin agreed to star in both productions and, as a result, led a brutal schedule the next eight months, showing real stamina and dedication.

The first deal was made official when Fox announced in *Daily Variety*, December 4, 1968, that Dustin would star opposite Mia Farrow in the screen version of *John and Mary*. The movie was to be based on Mervyn Jones's best-selling novel of the same title. Peter Yates, who one year earlier brought moviegoers *Bullitt* with Steve Mc-Queen, was signed to direct the film. Principal filming commenced on January 27, 1969, at the Biograph Studios and various other locations in New York. The movie was filmed while Dustin returned to Broadway to star in *Jimmy Shine*, which celebrated Dustin's first Broadway stage appearance since his critically acclaimed performance in *Eh?*

Dustin spent three long, tedious weeks learning his lines and immersing himself in his character for the show. By the time rehearsals were under way, he had most of his nuances and character foibles down pat—except for some shifts in moods of the character. These problems were quickly resolved before the show made its Broadway debut on Thursday, December 5, 1968, at New York's Brooks Atkinson Theatre. (The show was originally given a test run in Baltimore, Maryland, before coming to New York.)

Who was Jimmy Shine? Playwright Murray Schisgal imagined him as sort of a Benjamin Braddock-type, a young man searching vainly for a future. In fact, in many ways, Jimmy was nothing more than Benjamin reincarnated. Only this time, he was a high school student living in a warehouse rather than an upper-class mansion, such as in *The Graduate*. Some critics were referring to Jimmy as "a kind of Walter Mitty who lives in his own reveries." His means of solving these dreams were about as unpredictable as the dreams themselves. Suddenly, he might snap out of his world of fantasy and break into a song-and-dance routine, or do graphic impersonations of such Hollywood personalities as W. C. Fields. Moreover, he took up with a radical hippie group, hoping to find some answers there.

Once Jimmy no longer hungers for these unproductive relationships, he turns to art and find it's what he wants most in life. It is then that he strikes up a relationship with a hooker and poses her for a painting in a hotel room. A smile lights up his face as he realizes art is what he has been thirsting for all along. As much as art illustrates "an expression of growth," so do Jimmy's experiences hereafter.

Hoffman was convincing as the confused teen-ager but was unable to save the production from rampant criticism. Theater critics denounced the production and, in some cases, had very few kind words for Hoffman. As Richard P. Cooke, theater critic for *The Wall Street Journal*, wrote: "*Jimmy Shine* with its promising combination of talents proved disappointing to this reviewer. Perhaps just the presence of Mr. Hoffman may be enough for some playgoers, but it's not likely to be enough for everybody." *Newsweek* was less than pleasant, calling it "the baddest bad play possible to conceive . . . a mess, an incredibly hackneyed shamelessly exploitative farrago. . . . The play itself is a monster."

Although *Jimmy Shine* was bombarded with a high

volume of bad reviews, playwright Murray Schisgal was of the opinion that it might have been weaker without a true professional like Hoffman. "It's comfortable being with Dustin because he is always giving his all. I certainly don't think he ever shortchanged us in the production," Schisgal said.

As abysmal as the production was, however, Dustin had no room to complain. He was receiving forty-five hundred dollars a week and ten percent of the show's gross box-office receipts. Hoffman also picked up some loose change he wasn't counting on. Legend has it that the Broadway company didn't seek permission from Dustin to use certain materials featuring him in the show's theater programs. Upset, Hoffman held out for more money in the same manner baseball free agents hold out for bigger salaries. He bargained with show producer Zev Buffman and came away with half of the profits from every souvenir program sold. At one dollar a program, Dustin was reaping in as much as an extra one hundred dollars a week! Usually, income from program sales benefits the show's financial backers, but in this particular case, Hoffman's cut of the profits was a revolutionary move, indeed.

Dustin was not only a shrewd businessman but an equally shrewd manipulator of the people around him. Donald Driver, who directed *Jimmy Shine*, remembers: "He cut his finger on opening night in Baltimore. Long after it had healed, he insisted that the stage manager announce to the audience that Mr. Hoffman was appearing with a cut finger. It was a blatant bid for public sympathy."

Sympathy or not, Dustin's solid acting job in *Jimmy Shine* represented a historic first on how playwrighting had changed over the years. The play touched on such tender subjects as prostitution and marijuana-smoking hippies, something that had previously been glossed over in stage and film productions. Instead, Hollywood and Broadway's new attitude was to mirror the crucial issues and problems of society. Whether Dustin realized it or not, it was his film *The Graduate* that triggered decisions by movie and stage producers to make stories on hard-hitting cultural themes that were more risqué.

Therefore, by the late 1960s, gone were the days of ingenuous scriptwriting for films; the industry was catching up with the times. People were more keenly aware of certain problems in society—like prostitution and drugs—but didn't want to discuss them openly. Film producers, however, decided it was time someone did.

One such movie that dealt with prostitution and homosexuality was *Midnight Cowboy*, featuring Dustin Hoffman as a scruffy homosexual, Ratso Rizzo. Written by screenwriter Waldo Salt, the film was based on James Herlihy's best-selling novel. Producer Jerome Hellman and director John Schlesinger have said that adapting Herlihy's book was a long ordeal that they would rather forget.

As early as August 1965, when the novel was first published, movie agents had made the rounds to studios with the novel as a possible movie. Every major film studio, including United Artists (who produced the movie), turned down the book. United Artists' final report said that the action "goes steadily downhill." In October 1966, however, one year after the decision to take no action on the property, United Artists' president David V. Picker bought the movie rights to the novel. He then met with English director John Schlesinger and signed him to direct the picture, with Hellman producing.

When writing the film became a rather cumbersome

task, Schlesinger's agent tried persuading him to drop out of the project. He had the opportunity to pilot Jack Lemmon, Schlesinger's favorite actor, in *The April Fools*. That left Schlesinger in a quandary. He had just come off directing a disastrous foreign import, *Far from the Madding Crowd*, and wanted his next picture to be a hit. "I'd had a flop, which unnerved me a bit," Schlesinger recalls. "You're expected to have smash hits all the time in America. Frankly, that terrible old adage about only being as good as your last picture was totally the attitude, I'm afraid. I half-believed things people were saying and yet I also knew that *Midnight Cowboy* was a damn good project."

Schlesinger added that the first actor to receive the script was Hoffman, who accepted the role as the scrofulous Ratso Rizzo straightaway. Tests then began for the lead of Joe Buck, the swaggering cowboy who makes his fortune off sex-hungry women in New York. Four actors were tested, including Michael Sarrazin and Jon Voight.

Voight was a tall, blond, blue-eyed actor from New York. He had won a Theatre World award for his performance opposite Irene Papas in *That Summer, That Fall* and collected critical kudos for his portrayal of Rudolfo in Off-Broadway's *A View from the Bridge* (on which Hoffman had been assistant director). Voight had been featured in some films and, more notably, on such television shows as "Cimarron Strip" and "Gunsmoke." And Voight was no stranger to Hoffman.

Jon won the part as Buck hands down and filming began in April 1968. In order for Dustin to star in the film, Schlesinger was able to arrange his shooting schedule around Hoffman's matinee performances of *Jimmy Shine*. Schlesinger remarked: "Dustin made extraordinary sense the first time he ever read the script. He also seemed to have the right physical image to play Ratso. Jerry Hellman felt the same. Now I can't imagine anyone else playing Ratso." With Hoffman coming off the success of *The Graduate,* he was offered two hundred fifty thousand—or fifteen times what he earned for his first film—for his portrayal as Ratso.

The budget of *Midnight Cowboy* was originally set at $2 million. As is the case with most Hollywood blockbusters, however, filming extended past allotted schedule—as did the budget. United Artists seriously contemplated not sinking any more money into the production, since it was felt that the movie might not recoup its investment if the budget was extended.

United Artists officials held a conference to reconcile the issue. Legally, the standard provision in both filmmakers' contracts stated that if the initial budget was depleted, the company could gain back full control of the production. Strangely enough, the question of seizing control of the movie was never raised at the meeting. Instead, filming continued and was completed at the final cost of $3 million.

In the meantime, Dustin continued starring in *Jimmy Shine* until its close on April 26, 1969, after 161 consecutive performances. Around the time filming on *Midnight Cowby* began, Dustin took time to consider another of his personal ambitions. Up until then, by his own calculations, he had been in love seven times and had lived with two women. But now he was ready for a more stable and meaningful relationship.

The woman of his life was the tall, slender, brunet ballet dancer named Anne Byrne. Dustin had been courting Anne for three years, since his days as star of *The*

Graduate. Born and raised in Chappaqua, New York, Byrne attending Horace Greeley School before studying at the American School of Ballet.

During the years of their relationship, Anne was able to witness Dustin's growth as an actor and the blossoming of their love for each other. Likewise, Dustin was able to watch Anne improve as she pursued a part-time ballet career. Dustin always admitted that he liked women who were intellectually and creatively stimulating, and Anne definitely fell into that category. Although they were of opposite religions—Anne was Catholic, and Dustin Jewish—this never presented much of a problem. Often Dustin had contemplated marriage, but he wanted his career firmly entrenched before taking the marital plunge.

It was the first marriage for Dustin; Anne was divorced and had a daughter, Karina, by her first marriage. The ceremony took place on May 4, 1969, at Temple Beth El synagogue in northern Westchester, New York. About thirty-five close friends and relatives attended the wedding, including Hoffman's parents and brother, Ronald. After the wedding was over, the couple took off for a honeymoon retreat in Asia.

Back in Hollywood, pessimism grew within the ivory towers of United Artists' business office. Executives were arguing over whether *Midnight Cowboy* would recoup its investment, unless a highly concentrated promotional campaign was planned. The company decided to embark on a widespread media blitz—radio spots, television commercials, newspaper and magazine interviews with Hoffman and Voight, and full-page newspaper ads—hoping to lure young filmgoers.

Success came fast when *Midnight Cowboy* was released to selected theaters on May 26, 1969, with first-week box-office totals very encouraging. In its first two days at New York's Coronet Theatre, an all-time house record was set, surpassing *The Graduate*. The movie rolled up a whopping $7,568 on opening day and $7,658 the following day. By August, Hollywood trade papers were reporting that the box-office gross of *Midnight Cowboy* had reached $1,017,872. That included $491,233 in nine weeks in New York; $182,288 in almost five weeks in Boston; and $102,800 in Chicago. As United Artists' president David V. Picker recalls: "When we saw the film one afternoon, we were stunned by its magic and the magic of Hoffman and Voight together. So we decided on a special release pattern—an opening in New York a couple months before anywhere else, play-off in small theaters with long engagements, letting word of mouth build an audience."

Word of mouth and the film's X-rating were certainly key factors for *Midnight Cowboy*'s surprise box-office success, as well as the fact that Hoffman's legion of fans had grown. Adults were struck by Dustin's pathetic character, Ratso Rizzo, so much so that many returned to see the movie several times.

Midnight Cowboy will be one of the most talked about films throughout this century, dealing as it did, frankly and without restraint, with heterosexual and homosexual love. Jon Voight as Joe Buck, a gregarious cowboy stud who becomes a big-city hustler, models himself after male heroes of the western film. He dresses himself in the same fashion as his favorite screen idols—from Roy Rogers to John Wayne—and carries with him a picture of Paul Newman.

The film begins with a series of flashbacks of Buck recounting his life as an abandoned child on the doorstep of his grandmother's front porch. Later, the dream sequence segues to his first intimate relationship with his girl friend, Crazy Anne, who is gang-raped. Buck then recalls that Anne said he was the only one she had wanted. Sorrowful that his relationship was over and visibly bitter, he remarks, "Lovin' was all I was ever good for." With that statement, he presses his transistor radio to his ear and hops a bus bound for New York.

There, as a male hustler, he beds down with women of all shapes and all ages, most of whom are far more unfeeling than he. One scene spares no amount of realism of sexual lust, when a streetwalker (Sylvia Miles) gets so impatient that she unzips Buck's fly while she's talking on the telephone. Rather than collect his fee—Buck was charging women for his services—Miles manipulates Joe to reverse the charges.

In another scene, this time at a swinging party, an independent woman (Brenda Vaccaro), whom Buck views as just another body, seduces him. After a night of ecstasy, the girl passes his name around and, eventually, through word of mouth, Buck becomes a primary object of pursuit by other women. Their tricks—leaving him penniless and distraught—become so unpleasant that he decides that love and understanding might be found with another man.

Thus, his attachment to the scruffy, tubercular Ratso Rizzo emerges. In essense, the bond between Joe and Ratso is the coming together of losers rather than lovers. Only as the film progresses does their relationship become more poignant. (Dustin has said that there was some discussion over filming an actual sexual encounter between Ratso and Joe, but plans for the scene were scrapped at the last minute.) Director John Schlesinger, who makes this delicate subject matter work, avoids a sick or destructive view of the affection between these two men.

Ratso is particularly appealing—thanks largely to Hoffman's real-life portrayal of this pathetic character. As Ratso, Dustin shows a wide range of emotions—love, sympathy, realism, laughter, and sorrow—emotions that never came to fruition in his previous screen characters. Ratso also represents a misfit in society and an antihero of immeasurable qualities. As someone from the lowest stratum of life, he limps unsteadily downhill spitting blood, breaking into a cold sweat, and using the *New York Daily News* for underwear. Eventually, filmgoers learn that Ratso is dying.

In his closing moments, Ratso tells Buck what it means to be a man. He informs Joe that "cowboy stuff is strictly for fags." In defense, expecting Ratso to define cowboy masculinity, Buck remarks: "John Wayne—you want to tell me he's a fag?" Ratso maintains that all heroes, in their stoic manner, conceal sexual ambivalence and uneasiness with the outward display of heterosexuality.

The film ends with Joe and Ratso taking a bus trip to Florida to fulfill a dream of Ratso's. Showing his affection, Buck wipes Ratso's sweating brow and comforts him during the long trip. Sadly, Ratso's dream is never fully realized, as he dies in Buck's comforting arms. Joe's arms still around his dear friend, the music comes up in homage to Ratso.

Although Hoffman does a first-rate job of acting in *Midnight Cowboy*, the film clearly belongs to Jon Voight, who makes the film's homosexual subject matter come off as unoffensive and innocent. Schlesinger, rebounding from his flop *Far from the Madding Crowd*, employs a fine array of comic, poignant, and—on occasion—ugly and sordid episodes to paint a real picture of a homosexual's life. Even Waldo Salt's dramatic screen adaptation holds faithful to the sexual episodes that seemed daring and permissive in the book. Salt also packed into the script a surprisingly large number of incidents that were in the book, which is quite uncommon for most screenplay-novelization adaptations.

Midnight Cowboy put Schlesinger back on top of the heap and also put Voight in the limelight. Hoffman also benefited as major weekly magazines began carrying interviews with the actor, labeling him "Hollywood's Newest Antihero." After the release of *Midnight Cowboy*, Dustin revealed, however, that friends had tried discouraging him from taking on the role of Ratso. As he put it in an interview, "Some felt it would be a career mistake." But Hoffman was fascinated by Ratso, especially since he represented a person regarded in society "as the scum of the earth." He later added, however: "I wanted to get inside one of those people. They're really no different from us. Their circumstances are just different." In addition, Hoffman said he had nothing but high regard for the film and has often called it one of his favorites. "I just have a fondness for *Midnight Cowboy*. I came closer in that film to achieving the kind of work that is most personal to me," he said.

Critics agreed as they regarded the film "a revolutionary achievement." As *Hollywood Reporter* critic John Mahoney enthused: "Dustin Hoffman and Jon Voight head a large and outstanding cast in a film which will be one of the most discussed and profitable of the year." *Newsweek* offered even more encouraging words of praise: "Voight's performance is so good, though, that his presence compels belief in the past (Hoffman's work is in no way inferior, but the script gives the movie to Voight)." Meanwhile, *Look* magazine critic Gene Shalit reported that the movie was "a reeking masterpiece . . . an intense examination of a sick society."

A surprise review came from a most unlikely source, however: *Midnight Cowboy* author James Leo Herlihy. At a press conference in Hollywood, Herlihy told scores of reporters that he had never dreamed that "anyone would dare make a film" out of *Midnight Cowboy*. Herlihy stated that he had the same incredulous feelings studios were expressing while first considering it as a feature-length movie. "I had no interest in it because the word around Hollywood was that it was going to be a bomb," Herlihy recalled. "When I went to the premiere in New York— then I got interested."

It is commonly popular for novelists to condemn film versions of their works, but Herlihy's enthusiastic comments were truly genuine. "I absolutely loved it—most of it. John Schlesinger was marvelous and Waldo Salt was fantastic. Dustin Hoffman was perfect as Ratso."

Midnight Cowboy continued drawing filmgoers of all adult ages and collecting handily at the box office. Although the film was released late that spring, it still qualified for Academy Award consideration. So when Hollywood's annual Oscar ceremonies were held in April 1969, *Midnight Cowboy* was nominated for best picture, best actor, and best director. Hoffman and Voight shared best actor nominations, Hoffman for the second time.

To the delight of Wayne fans all across America, the Duke stole the best actor sweepstakes from Hoffman and Voight for his sterling performance as a rugged cowboy in *True Grit*. As a token, *Midnight Cowboy* took best picture and Schlesinger best director. Despite those two awards, Hoffman and Voight felt slighted, and this second defeat fed Dustin's sour feelings about the Academy Awards.

Shrugging it off, Hoffman began concentrating his energies on another film, *Little Big Man*. Budgeted as an epic western, the film was to feature Dustin as Jack

Crabb, the sole survivor of Custer's Last Stand. The film went before the cameras in the spring of 1970.

Meanwhile, United Artists was expanding its release of *Midnight Cowboy* nationwide, including its first run in Los Angeles. UA studio officials were eager to cash in on the aftereffects of the film's two Oscars. By the time *Midnight Cowboy* came to Hollywood, however, another Hoffman movie was being readied for distribution: Twentieth Century-Fox's *John and Mary*.

Before the film began production, Dustin remarked that he had taken on the part of John not because of the script but as a favor to director Peter Yates. "When we were in Baltimore trying out *Jimmy Shine*, we were in terrific trouble, and Peter came down two or three times and sat up all night with us and made some excellent suggestions," Dustin once recalled. "He seemed more involved in helping the play than with planning the movie, and I thought, 'This is a real genuine guy.'"

There were other motives. Dustin had followed *The Graduate* with a gimpy-legged pimp in Ratso Rizzo, a character behind a mask of makeup. John was a challenge because it would mark the first time Dustin had taken on a lead role since *The Graduate*, and also his first romantic screen role. Hoffman saw portraying a romantic character like John as a way to expand his horizons, even though he hadn't been considered much of a lover in *The Graduate*.

John and Mary focuses on the trials and tribulations of a bachelor named John (Dustin Hoffman) who meets a single girl named Mary (Mia Farrow) in a Manhattan singles bar. They adjourn to John's apartment for a weekend of sex and of testing each other as candidates for an affair, without even catching each other's name. As it turns out, Mary has already been taking delight in a sexual affair with a married politician; John is not fazed, and proceeds to make advances on her. As John confesses following his first sexual encounter with Mary, "If it's going to be serious, it's gotta be right."

The film then takes a twist, examining the attitudes, fears, and fantasies of the two characters in need of good reasons to stay with each other. Hoffman shows his shrewdness as an actor in capably bringing off his role as a contemporary romantic lead. He comes across on the screen as sincere, caring, and sensual in many of the scenes with his new love. Mia Farrow, on the other hand, demonstrates her sexual prowess as well as her ability to handle a serious dramatic role.

Eventually they fall in love with each other, but John is hesitant at first to commit himself to a relationship. He can only reflect on his one bad experience with his former live-in model, Ruth (Sunny Griffin), who cluttered his life with personal tragedies and his apartment with her untidiness. Nevertheless, John gradually convinces himself that he can trust Mary as that "right girl in his life" and asks her to move in with him. In the closing moments of the film, John, elated over his final decision to win her, hops in bed with Mary for another sexual go-round. It's during this final lustful encounter that Mary queries, "My name is Mary . . . What about you?"

Director Peter Yates's sensitive direction enables the film to communicate tenderness and emotion, even though it fails to liven up an otherwise dull story. Gayne Rescher's stunning photography adds to the intensity of the many intimate love scenes between John and Mary. And Hoffman remains in top form, although at times he appears nervous in his new antihero role. The film's only major fault, however, stems from the screenplay written by John Mortimer, which comes off at times as clumsy and illogical. It seems absurd that two people wouldn't have introduced themselves to each other until several weeks of jumping into bed together have passed. The same denseness permeates the film's theme of the untrustworthiness of women.

Fox was viewing *John and Mary* as a revival of an old studio practice—merging prominent male and female stars to draw big box office. Film producer Ben Kadish was hoping to live up to the tradition originally made famous in teaming such Hollywood giants as Jimmy Stewart and June Allyson, Spencer Tracy and Katharine Hepburn, Rock Hudson and Doris Day, and, of course, Mickey Rooney and Judy Garland. Critics were vastly disappointed with the studio's inability to create a solid, convincing script, rather than a theatrical diversion for these two up-and-coming film stars. As *Newsweek* so strongly remarked: "The size of the dialogue and performances is wrong. It's American-size intimacy that suffers from the problems of American compact cars: too big to be nimble and too small to be impressive."

Defending the movie's sporadic finer qualities, *Hollywood Reporter* enthused over Hoffman's performance as John: "Hoffman gives yet another outstanding performance, uniquely communicating subsurfaced emotions, without the benefit of interior dialogue. It is a performance of subtle clarity, intimate, enriched by humor and tenderness, proving that he can play a contemporary romantic leading role. . . ." *Time* magazine wasn't as generous with its compliments: "*John and Mary* is as empty as a singles bar on Monday morning. Leaning on the stars' reputation, it never bothers to show who the lovers are, or how they got to be that way."

John and Mary made its first run in Hollywood on November 25, 1969, during Thanksgiving week, and on the same day box-office figures for the Los Angeles screen engagement of *Midnight Cowboy* were released. In five days at the Bruin Theatre in Westwood, *Midnight Cowboy* had grossed a whopping $14,118, while *John and Mary* started off sluggishly.

Dustin was visibly disappointed over the film's lack of success at the box office and with the reviews. Later he admitted his doubts about handling a romantic role such as John. He once said that he found his emotions weren't coming to surface in a one-dimensional character like John, even though many fans and some critics would disagree.

Dustin wasn't expecting any additional bumps in his career when his second flop of the year took to screens nationwide. His role as the bumbling U.S. Treasury man in the low-budget comedy *Madigan's Millions* was finally distributed theatrically in America two years after production had been completed in Italy. (The film, released on December 29, 1969, was produced in 1967 following Dustin's first film appearance in Columbia Pictures' *The Tiger Makes Out*.)

Madigan's Millions, which costarred Cesar Romero and Latin bombshell Elsa Martinelli, was double-billed in the United States with another oldie but moldie, *Fearless Frank*, starring Jon Voight in his pre-*Midnight Cowboy* days. Actually, *Madigan's Millions* couldn't have been released at a better time (at least for the producer), since the film generated some hefty box-office revenue—thanks in large to Hoffman's gainful popularity.

Madigan's Millions is a comedy-drama (believe it or not!) concerning Mike Madigan (Cesar Romero), an Italian hood, who has escaped from the United States to Rome after stealing a million dollars. In standard Mafia-style, he is murdered (two minutes into the film), and the Italian and American embassies are very interested in re-covering the money. So the Treasury Department dis-patches its top Washington aide, Jason Fister (Dustin Hoffman). This results in a kaleidoscope of events in which Hoffman runs into trouble with the Italian police, with gangsters, becomes involved in two murders, aids the lovely Elsa Martinelli, and clumsily recovers the money (breaking Hoffman's tradition of starring in anti-hero roles).

The film was far from a critical masterpiece. Probably the funniest sequence in the film is the opening one, which features an animated Dustin Hoffman driving over a puzzle board of booby traps. Typical of Italian comedy fare, Hoffman mugs endlessly, as do his Latin contempo-raries. The entire cast of actors, except for Dustin, is poorly dubbed, adding to the utter hilarity of this hap-less little seventy-seven-minute film. James Henaghan's screenplay is lukewarm, perhaps the result of too much pasta, and Stanley Prager's direction shows even less promise.

An even less supporting legion of critics turned up their noses on *Madigan's Millions*, including *Hollywood Re-porter*, which observed: ""Fortunately for Dustin Hoff-man, the film which introduced him to the world was not the film which introduced him to the screen. . . . The Latin cast is awful, mugging inanely so that the dubbed voices couldn't help even if they were better." A critic for *Film Daily* showed his audacity in remaining faithful to Hoffman when he remarked: "No doubt about it, Dustin Hoffman is talented. He is so naïve, nutty, clumsy, and talented in *Madigan's Millions* that he is the whole film. In fact, he saves the film."

Despite the financial flops—*John and Mary* and *Madigan's Millions*—Hoffman knew that things had to look up. His only question was, "When?"

5

New Roles

Little Big Man . . .
and becoming a father

Aware of the Hollywood adage that "an actor is as good as his last picture," Dustin was hoping something better was in store. It came: the follow-up role of an irritable 122-year-old man named Jack Crabb, claiming to be the sole survivor of Custer's Last Stand in Arthur Penn's epic western, *Little Big Man.*

The movie had been in the making for some time. MGM had originally planned on producing the film as a multimillion-dollar property, based on Thomas Berger's best-selling novel. Somehow the deal at Metro fell through, and in June 1969, a lesser-known studio, Cinema Center Films, agreed to finance the film. Jack Richardson, who had started writing the screenplay, was replaced by one of Hoffman's favorite screenwriters, Calder Willingham (who wrote *The Graduate*). The film was originally set to be produced on a budget of $5 million with Dustin in the title role and was to be filmed at such diverse locations as Los Angeles, Billings, Montana, Colorado, Custer's Battlefield, Nevada City, and Calgary, Canada.

Although Hoffman was anxious to redeem his screen image, he wasn't so anxious to leave his wife, Anne, and daughter, Karina, alone. He was very sensitive about others, especially when it came to his family. He didn't enjoy traveling for extended periods of time unless his family was along with him. His cure: He invited his wife and daughter to join him, and made it customary with each production that followed. This problem settled, Hoffman set out with producer Stuart Millar and associate producer Gene Lasko for the start of production on *Little Big Man*. His costars were actress Faye Dunaway as a bawdy frontier belle and Chief Dan George, among the Indians selected for major roles (George replaced Richard Boone in the role of the seventy-year-old Chief Old Lodge Skins).

Hoffman has recalled that *Little Big Man* created its share of problems with the American Indians. Stuart Millar had to sign a treaty permitting the use of Custer's Last Stand battlefield in the movie. The agreement had one catch: Millar had to employ about forty Crow Indians in the film. Similar agreements were drawn up with the Northern Cheyenne to film scenes at Lame Deer, Montana, and with Scarvee and Stony Indians for the use of land in Calgary. Hoffman remarked also that Millar approved of these agreements as a means of strengthening relations with the Indians and warding off protests against the film as "denigrating to Indians."

Filming was postponed temporarily because of unbearable weather conditions. In Calgary, temperatures plummeted to fifty degrees below zero. Despite the bitter climate, however, director Arthur Penn's 114-man cast and crew proceeded on schedule with filming—well, almost on schedule. Actually, bad weather conditions put the production so far behind that Hoffman has said that Penn's expenditures totaled $10 million, doubling the picture's original budget.

According to Dustin, the most disconcerting aspect of his role as Jack Crabb was creating a voice old enough to match his character. As he told magazine reporter Richard Meryman in an interview: "I first tried to get that kind of raspy voice that comes when the vocal chords have broken down. A doctor friend of mine found this home on Welfare Island where I could just observe old people. I found one guy and talked to him for a while on tape. He wasn't right—just wasn't old enough—and I was very depressed afterward. Then, another doctor told me there was a drug that dries out alcoholics and makes something very raspy happen to the voice. But I chickened out."

Dustin's next stop was Montana to continue filming, even though the upcoming scenes as the old man were still haunting him, since he was not set on a particular voice. "Then, one day I got laryngitis, and I practiced with it, played the voice back on tape," Hoffman said. "It was exactly what I wanted. But then I thought, 'What am I going to do? Get sick?' Finally, we were in Canada, in the fifth month of the picture, and I got friendly with an Oriental fellow who was one hundred four years old. Here I had gone through Montana looking through different rest homes to find the right guy, and here he was sitting right in front of me. So I went back for four hours and just watched him."

Dustin didn't have to use his old man's voice until filming resumed in Los Angeles. When the production shifted back to the West Coast, however, Hoffman panicked the day before shooting because he lost the kind of gravelly voice he had been working on. "I still didn't know what to do about the voice. So in a panic I went into a room, closed the door, and started screaming until I got hoarse. The next day my voice was okay again. So I screamed while I got dressed, I screamed leaving the room. In the car I rolled up the windows and screamed all the way to the Sawtelle Veteran's Hosital. I screamed vowel sounds and different registers, screamed do, re, me, fa, trying to find a register more delicate than the others that would get hoarser." Dustin was fortunate: the screaming worked.

Equally memorable to Hoffman was the time spent under the hot, steaming makeup lamps being trans-formed into the 122-year-old Jack Crabb. A fourteen-piece mask that took five hours to create was applied to his face. The mask was the creation of Hollywood's legend-ary makeup artist Dick Smith. Hoffman later quipped, "I defy anyone to put on that makeup and not feel old."

Because of the new wrinkles, Hoffman has recalled that the crew unconsciously started treating him like an elderly man. "I couldn't see too well with my contact lens cataracts, and they'd walk me over to the wheelchair where they had to wheel me, and everybody was very gentle. That really helped me believe my fantasy world."

By late November, Dustin's "fantasy world" was finished, production of *Little Big Man* was completed, and editing began on the film back in Hollywood. In the meantime, Dustin took a well-deserved rest between en-gagements to spend time with his family in New York. Having been on location the last five months, Hoffman was counting the days when he didn't have to battle the rat race of a shooting schedule to enjoy the company of his wife and daughter. Hanukkah was also drawing near, although Dustin didn't relish the celebration of the traditional religious holiday. As he said recently, "I'm not the least bit religious. I have never been."

Hoffman made news again in 1970, wheeling and dealing himself into a picture deal with the irrepressible film producer Franco Zeffirelli. Zeffirelli, newspapers reported, was trying to land Hoffman in the lead of *Brother Sun and Sister Moon,* a film Paramount Pictures had dropped. But Zeffirelli, whose *Romeo and Juliet* had been the surprise hit of the year before, denied the reports. The actor's representatives at the William Morris Agency, meanwhile, were admitting that Hoffman had conversed with Zeffirelli but that no deal had been struck. A few days later rumors were revived when Dustin edged toward signing with Zeffirelli. But his interest in the project suddenly went stale.

Actually, Dustin was caught between the decision to engage himself in another film property or return to Broadway. Hoffman had always had a soft spot in his heart for the immediacy of New York stage productions whereas films take longer to produce.

Then, in March 1970, Dustin reappeared in newspaper and magazine pages across the country, but not with the news of a new role. Headlines instead were screaming out news that three sharp blasts had rung out from the street in Greenwich Village where Dustin was living. The explosion set fire to Hoffman's Federal-style house and destroyed many of his private possessions. Fortunately, at the time of the explosion, Dustin, Anne, and Karina had left for downtown New York.

When Dustin heard the news of the blaze, he rushed to the scene. He was able to pull from the smoke-filled home three of his modern paintings and a Tiffany lampshade. Sadly, the rest of his collection of paintings and furniture had been badly charred or destroyed. All told, twenty-three people were left homeless from blasts, and at the time police were unable to find suspects responsible for setting off the explosions. As Dustin told friends afterward, "Thank God, I'm not poor!"

Shortly after the incident, Dustin was signed to star in another feature film for Cinema Center Films—his second for the studio—called *Who Is Harry Kellerman and Why Is He Saying Those Terrible Things About Me?* Hoffman's old Broadway chum Ulu Grosbard was brought in to direct the screenplay by Herb Gardner (who had won an Oscar nomination the year before for his screenplay of *A Thousand Clowns*).

Harry Kellerman was set practically in Hoffman's backyard, one of the few films not to inconvenience the actor with a hectic out-of-state traveling schedule. Filming of Hoffman's scenes took place in many downtown New York locations, including a Fifth Avenue penthouse overlooking Central Park, the BMT subway in Brooklyn, the Lincoln Tunnel, Coney Island, the Lunt-Fontanne Theatre; and a special sequence was filmed at the famed Manhattan rock palace, Fillmore East. Scenes of Dustin in his duplex were filmed high atop the fiftieth floor of the General Motors Building.

Hoffman's least favorite scene was one that took place in front of the General Motors Building. It called for him to enter the structure while a growing crowd of fans cheered him on (he's billed as a rock star in the film). The temperamental actor Hoffman can sometimes be was vehemently against the idea of a live audience at first, and he protested loudly, but after he walked through the scene once, Grosbard convinced him how vital the segment was to the film. Hoffman later admitted that he was rather uncomfortable performing before a live audience—especially "an audience of gawking fans!" He kept his head down while walking through the jeering throng so as not to let it break his concentration.

Throughout his career, Dustin has been an advocate of his own theories of movie-making. He was unafraid to speak his piece with directors or provide input into writers' screenplays, preferring to control the situation; that way, the character was really his. Some directors have complained about Dustin's infringement on their own creativity, but the vast majority of directors encouraged it. In interjecting his own ideas into a specific character or scene, Hoffman was following not only the example of other actors but also his own intuition, since he seemed to know his own ability best.

Harry Kellerman was Dustin's first film since *Little Big Man*, a vehicle that he felt was much more in line with his own capabilities. In a newspaper interview, Hoffman related that up until *Harry Kellerman* he was fairly satisfied with his career. As he remarked, "In some ways, I am [satisified]. I made one mistake and that was *John and Mary*. I was aware that it wasn't working. It wasn't the director's fault. But I had no tie-in with the character. It's not such a bad feeling to fail in something you feel connected with, but just being unable to make it is. To fail in something you are connected with can be upsetting, though."

Dustin also maintains that he felt comfortable working with Grosbard as his director. His friendship with Ulu dated back to 1962 when he had been a character actor for the Theatre Company of Boston; the first show Dustin did for the company— *Waiting for Godot*—was directed by Grosbard. Later he rejoined Grosbard on Broadway as assistant director for *A View from the Bridge*.

Even in the midst of production on *Harry Kellerman*, Dustin had been hearing other film offers. The one that caught his eye was the narration of an animated feature that Murkami-Wolf Productions was producing for ABC-TV, called *The Point*. The feature was based on a story by Harry Nilsson, with music also provided by the famed songwriter, and was broadcast as part of ABC's "Movie of the Week" series on February 2, 1971. Dustin was not only the narrator but as a storyteller played the part of a suburban father competing with the television set for his disinterested kid's attention.

Meanwhile, Hoffman continued with filming of *Harry Kellerman* until completion in early October. Dustin was fortunate that filming didn't run overtime, especially during the second week of October. Hoffman's wife, Anne, had given up her career as a part-time dancer some months earlier because the stresses of pregnancy were becoming extremely wearing. Dustin was at Anne's side when she gave birth on October 15, 1970, to their second child, Jennifer Celia (nicknamed Jenna), who weighed in at eight pounds, three ounces. The birth of Jennifer made Dustin deeply grateful; he not only had the perfect wife but the perfect family. Ironically, it was the second celebration Dustin had had in as many days. The day before Anne went into labor, he signed a lucrative contract to star in one of his most ambitious film projects to date: Sam Peckinpah's *Straw Dogs*. Filming wasn't to commence until later that year, giving him plenty of time to get to know his newborn daughter.

Some time after Jennifer's birth, in late November, Dustin was invited to attend a luncheon in New York sponsored by the American Jewish Committee's Motion Picture and Entertainment Division. Over five hundred motion-picture directors and producers gathered to pay tribute to Dustin, who had been nominated winner of the department's annual William J. German Human Relations Award. Gordon T. Stulberg, president of Cinema Center Films, presented the award to Dustin and cited him for his work to "further human understanding to achieve a better society through the political process." Hoffman had long been a supporter of the New York Psychoanalytic Institute, and it was for this that he was being honored. Previous recipients of the award included many of Dustin's Hollywood contemporaries: Sidney Poitier, Stanley Kramer, Paul Newman, and Joanne Woodward.

Dustin's string of good news continued when National General Pictures released *Little Big Man* to the screen on December 14, 1970, opening first at New York's Paramount and Sutton theaters, and was greeted by good reviews. Since it ran almost two and a half hours, some critics complained that the film was too long. But fans didn't seem to mind. The movie struck up brisk business the first couple of weeks with no visible cooling trend in sight. Fans lined the boulevards of many New York theaters, a first for Hoffman. And Dustin was attracting teen-agers as well, all flocking to catch a glimpse of Hollywood's newest "wonder boy." *The Graduate* and *Midnight Cowboy* were merely stepping-stones; *Little Big Man* was the film that put him over the top to stay.

Flashback-style, our story opens with a frail, raspy-voiced 122-year-old Jack Crabb, at last count the only surviving member of Custer's Last Stand, recounting the trials and tribulations of a fruitful life. He vividly recalls that at age ten, the Cheyenne Indians captured him and that Chief Old Lodge Skins (Chief Dan George) adopted him and raised him as a brave. This historic accounting of his early life takes on a new twist when Crabb, fifteen, is rescued by the white people and is taken under the care of the Reverend Mr. Pendrake (Thayer Davis) and his oversexed wife (Faye Dunaway), who provides the film's comic relief as owner of a brothel. As Crabb grows up, his life encompasses two wives, bankruptcy, alcoholism, and careers as an Indian scout and con artist.

The film's most dramatic moments splash onto the screen when General Custer makes the ill-fated decision to take over the territory of Little Bighorn. Similar to the classic shoot-'em-up westerns, Custer's regiment of soldiers charges right into an Indian camp, consisting of hundreds of Indians, enough to outnumber his small army of men. The ensuing massacre is as authentic and bloody as history books record. Crabb survives the bloodbath, mourning the death of his wife and child, who were killed in the Indian crossfire (Crabb was married to three Indian squaws).

Hoffman's portrayal of Jack Crabb shows signs of Ben Braddock and Ratso Rizzo combined, depending on the period of Crabb's life of course. It was another sparkling performance as a proficient antihero. His characterization of Crabb is one of a survivor of a slaughter that should have never been. Dustin demonstrates also his ability to make filmgoers believe in him as the crusty 122-year-old Crabb; through many mannerisms of the old— the constant wiping of the brow with a handkerchief and the methodical, gravelly speech pattern.

A competent troupe of supporting players also turned in fine performances, including Chief Dan George as Crabb's Indian mentor, Jeff Corey as Wild Bill Hickock, Richard Mulligan as General Custer, Thayer Davis as the Reverend Pendrake, and Faye Dunaway as the preacher's prostitute wife.

The film comes off more as true documentary than as western genre, primarily because of the pace. The film's 147-minute length slows down the story of Crabb's flash-

back, since there are too many episodic scenes throughout the picture. Some of the film's other problems are
incongruous scriptwriting and a diffused and rambling
direction. Calder Willingham tries cramming too many
ideas into his screenplay, while director Arthur Penn
does little to make the film more compact.

Despite some of the film's glaring flaws, critics were
nearly unanimous in their critical kudos of Hoffman in
the role of Jack Crabb, agreeing that the film evidenced
Hoffman's versatility and his enormous acting range. As
Hollywood Reporter critic Larry Cohen wrote of Dustin: "It
is a virtuoso performance demonstrating a refined sense
of several different kinds of comedy, age, and serious-
ness. He acquits himself admirably, and it's good to see
him in such a demanding enterprise." Vincent Canby, a
critic for *The New York Times*, called the film "most extrav-
agant and ambitious," while *The Los Angeles Times* critic
Charles Champlin said that Hoffman as Jack Crabb "was
blindingly vivid and showy." Clearly, Hoffman was in
the driver's seat again.

6

Branching Out
Straw Dogs; Harry Kellerman; Alfredo, Alfredo

Talk in Hollywood was that Dustin deserved an Oscar. *Little Big Man* was becoming a huge box-office success for Hoffman and for Cinema Center Films, and Dustin began moving up a couple of notches in popularity polls across the country.

The film was one of the first epic Hollywood westerns in nearly a decade. John Wayne was still among the leading box-office draws in America, with a virtual newcomer to films, Burt Reynolds, running a close second. Dustin wasn't trailing the pack by much, since his appeal with each film was strengthening.

Some actors struggle for fifteen years before breaking into that golden circle of Hollywood box-office giants. Dustin's controversial and explosive film performances were undoubtedly what pushed him into the limelight much sooner. *The Graduate,* replete with sexual and social overtones, established him as one of America's "brightest newcomers." His performance as Benjamin Braddock, however, pales in significance when compared to his

roles in *Midnight Cowboy* and *Little Big Man*, which really
bolted him to the top.

With his career picking up speed, Dustin started production of his sixth film, a classic Sam Peckinpah bloodbath called *Straw Dogs*. The film was being produced by
Dan Melnick and partners David Susskind and Leonard
Stern of Talent Associates. (Talent Associates was the
same company responsible for producing TV's long-run-
ning detective comedy series, "Get Smart.") The movie,
which started production February 3, 1971, was just one
of about a half-dozen features being produced exclusively
for ABC's new theatrical movie company.

British lovely Susan George was cast opposite Dustin
as his wife, with Peckinpah directing for ABC Pictures.
Straw Dogs required Dustin to board a plane for England,
where filming took place during a ten-week period. The
film had been adapted from Gordon M. Williams's best-
selling novel, *The Siege of Trencher's Farm* (the film's original title), and was based on a screenplay by David Z.
Goodman and Peckinpah.

Peckinpah's instinct for realism has been known to
result in graphic displays of violence in his films. Legend
has it that Peckinpah was also known to end arguments
by using his fists, even against women. These incidents
and disputes must have prompted producers to boycott
Peckinpah earlier from film-making for seven years.

He once recalled how he planned on indoctrinating
Hoffman and George. "I wanted to rub their noses in the
violence of it [the film]." In the midst of filming one day,
Hoffman recalled that Peckinpah drove himself and his
crew to the limits of endurance keeping them up half of
the night, as he was never satisfied with the outcome of
one take. According to Dustin, several technical crew
members grew tired enough of the long hours to cause

an all-out war with Peckinpah. Once the fight was over, Peckinpah decided to show everyone else he meant business, firing the two men. On another occasion, Susan George balked at playing a rape scene all the way to the end. Peckinpah, sparing no amount of realism, pulled George aside and brought in a buxom double to complete the scene.

These were some of the consequences of working with Peckinpah. His style of direction was unlike anyone else's in Hollywood, and as some stories have indicated, Peckinpah wasn't that well-respected by his peers. Dustin has admitted that working for Peckinpah was "a tough experience. But I loved working with him. He had the spontaneity of a child. Suddenly he would come up with things that were very exciting," which, according to Hoffman, made the filming of *Straw Dogs* that much more memorable.

The film was completed several months later, with principal editing beginning in Hollywood. Dustin came away from the film with a newfound feeling. He firmly believed in Peckinpah's enormous power as a director and had complete trust in the film enhancing his career. With the Peckinpah production now behind him, Dustin returned to his Greenwich Village home, where his wife and daughters awaited.

Occasionally, Hoffman broke out to work at his production office, Sweet Wall Productions, on West Fifty-sixth Street, which was located in the same building as Alan King's suite. He began restricting any personal appearances also, in order to have more time with his family. Then, in March 1971, Hollywood started putting the final trimmings on its annual Academy Award sweepstakes. Dustin was certainly hoping that *Little Big Man* would be nominated, as well as his performance for best actor. When he wasn't, he virtually exploded, taking out his vengeance on the Academy Awards' board of directors through the local media.

Hoffman related to his good friend and *Daily Variety* columnist, Army Archerd, that while he had been truly upset over not winning for *The Graduate* and *Midnight Cowboy*, he was feeling even more numb at the snubbing of his performance in *Little Big Man*. As he remarked in an interview with Archerd, "Sure I would like to win an Academy Award. I realize that intellectually it doesn't really mean very much. But it is a means to more power, which in turn enables you to be choosy about your scripts. And it makes you more money—which you can put away toward the day when you won't be in such demand!"

Another one of Dustin's aspirations was to play Adolf Hitler. "I'd really like to play him and I *could* play him, I think. But I'd also like to be a director. That way you can *really* be Hitler," Dustin quipped. In another interview, this time with syndicated columnist Dorothy Manners, Hoffman revived his longtime ambition to play Hitler. One of his friends, who was also present during the interview, commented: "Dustin is aware it would be very difficult to play Hitler. He sees it as a study in human as well as inhuman behavior—meaning the man behind the monster. His very words to me were, 'I have always attempted to see Hitler as a human being, an enigma who had enormous theatrical power and a sort of evil charm that seduced an entire nation.'"

Dustin remarked also to his friend that the film would have to have a great deal of present significance, and added that to examine Hitler would be a dramatic and political experience, which he described as "an explosive undertaking." Even though Hoffman was evidently set on portraying Hitler, film producers weren't as keen on the idea.

Although Dustin's plan to essay the role of Hitler was still in the planning stages, his film role in *Who Is Harry Kellerman and Why Is He Saying Those Terrible Things About Me?* was being released to theaters nationwide. Dustin was making very few tours, as the promotion for the film was primarily through newspaper and television interviews. *Harry Kellerman* brought to the screen a character role unlike any Hoffman had done before, and it put Hoffman out in front of the camera without the mask of makeup.

Harry Kellerman is a fantasy-comedy-drama intermingling reality with the shattering of the American dream for rock composer Georgie Soloway (Dustin Hoffman). He is unable to cope with the problems of life, despite his celebrity status as a top rock star, and tries jumping out of the window of his fiftieth-floor penthouse as the answer. His suicide leap turns into a dream, and he tries to rewrite his suicide note as he plummets to the pavement below.

When he awakens, he tries another solution: his psychiatrist, Dr. Solomon F. Moses (Jack Warden). Soloway's constant questioning on "Why is life so terrible?" eventually uncorks Dr. M., who suddenly bursts out singing "Leave Me Alone." Moses finally finishes his song and starts asking Georgie to recall the origin of his problems, stemming from childhood to the present. In flashback, Soloway begins remembering what his troubled life was like at eighteen years of age, up until his present age of forty.

Temporarily relieved of his anxiety, Soloway exits Dr. Moses's office and meets up with a female counterpoint, Allison Densmore (Barbara Harris), a psychotic girl who's auditioning for a stage job. She is just as disturbed, failing her audition when she is unable to free her hands from a lampstand. Georgie takes Allison under his wing, and right into his bed, where they do work out some of their frustrations.

In *Harry Kellerman*, Dustin is able to convey his agility and wide range of emotions as a prominent rock star-turned-society loser. Dustin certainly delivers in his portrayal, even though director Ulu Grosbard and screenwriter Herb Gardner do not. Grosbard fails to fully explain from the outset the reason for Soloway's mental problems, and never properly defines the reason for his suffering. Gardner, on the other hand, has pieced together a hodgepodge of inconsequential episodes that oftentimes make little sense.

Critics agreed in their appraisal of *Harry Kellerman*. As a critic for *Time* magazine remarked: "Like many rock concerts, *Harry Kellerman* has about 15 minutes of entertainment and hours to kill . . . the pictorial trickery cannot disguise the vapidity of the film." *Box Office* magazine, a popular Hollywood trade paper, commented that *Harry Kellerman* "is generally interesting despite an uneven quality." *Los Angeles Times* critic Charles Champlin, though, called Hoffman's performance as the sympathetic Georgie Soloway "a crackling and original work . . . another knockout performance." *Harry Kellerman* stole no honors during the year of its release, failing miserably at the box office. It was one of Dustin's first film disasters in some time.

But as he licked his wounds, his agent was fielding all kinds of new offers. One was from a new independent film comany called First Artists Productions, which was interested in releasing productions starring Hoffman and was willing to offer him creative control. Dustin's agent tried negotiating palatable terms while Hoffman was busy reading a new script.

The script was for the film *Till Divorce Do You Part*, a satirical comedy being produced and directed by Italian film maker Pietro Germi. Germi was known in America for his prizewinning comedy, *Divorce Italian Style*. The Latin film director was offering Dustin the lead, in addition to making him co-producer. Germi spiced up the offer with the promise that if Hoffman accepted the job of co-producer, he would have equal say on how his role was to be played. Dustin agreed to the deal and cameras began rolling on this Italian production that October. It was the first foreign import for Hoffman since his ill-fated comedy, *Madigan's Millions*.

Till Divorce Do You Part was originally to be spoken in Italian; since Dustin didn't know the language, he took a crash course. Germi, however, backed down on his decision to dub the picture because, in his words, "It is impossible for an Italian film, no matter how great, to play the general circuits in a dubbed version. America has accepted all the great foreign literary works in translated form, but has inexplicably denied the same treatment to motion pictures."

Germi decided instead to have Dustin act in his native tongue, because of "the traditional stupidity of the U.S. market that refused dubbed films." Some filmmakers, needless to say, started accusing Germi of signing Hoffman strictly for the reason of selling his comedy film to the United States. He later defended himself, remarking, "I did not offer Dustin the role as insurance for American release. I thought he was perfect for the story and sent him a script with about as much hope as those who put messages in bottles and toss them in the ocean."

Germi wasn't as exuberant about the movie's title, however, afraid that it might give audiences the impression that the film was a sequel to his previous hit, *Divorce Italian Style*. As a result, Germi retitled the film *Alfredo, Alfredo*.

Hoffman found that film-making in Italy was like living in another world. As he once said, "The pace is very leisurely. Germi knows exactly what he wants and cuts as he goes along. He doesn't have to take as many shots and gives more time to each one he wants. Everyone around him is like a member of the family. He's worked with them for years. I was the only newcomer to his unit and felt like a new boarder in a rooming house until I settled in."

Hoffman returned to the United States after completion of *Alfredo, Alfredo,* around the first week of February. Several months later, Dustin learned that Paramount Pictures had acquired the rights to distribute it in the United States and Canada.

As Dustin began to relax from the tension-filled filming, his fans were eagerly awaiting the premiere of his latest epic, *Straw Dogs*. The film made it screen debut on November 26, 1971, at Manhattan's Sutton Theater and was lauded by critics across the globe as "one of Peckinpah's best." Some critics also commended Peckinpah for supervising "a difficult and sometimes cloudy picture," while another army of critics credited Hoffman for making the picture hold up with another gleaming performance.

Straw Dogs combines an orgy of violence and nastiness with sexual repression, in a story of a quiet American mathematician, David Sumner (Dustin Hoffman), and his lively, sexy wife, Amy (Susan George). The couple move to an old farmhouse, Trencher's Farm, seeking privacy near Cornwall Village, where Amy had been born and raised.

David is an intellectual type who gets very little thrills from overt displays of sexual acts and violence. Amy, his complete opposite, is flirtatious and delights in enticing any man lusting for a night of sexual abandon—providing her husband's none the wiser. Eventually, an ex-lover from the village, along with one of his hooligan pals, gang-rapes Amy, who is too ashamed to apprise David of the rape, since she sort of liked it. It appears that her constant delight in flaunting herself starts making the farmhands resentful, too. Soon they begin taking every opportunity to humiliate David—from driving him off the road to strangling Amy's cat—gradually turning their vengeful fun into a bloodbath.

The high point of these violent acts comes to fruition when David helps a feebleminded villager, Henry Niles, who has accidentally killed an oversexed daughter of one of the villagers. Unaware that Niles has killed someone, David lets Niles take refuge in his farm, while the villagers become inflamed and stomp on his farm with guns and other weaponry, ready for murder. David, however, resists the villagers' siege of his farm and Niles, fighting them off with his own arsenal of weapons—an iron pipe, boiling water, cooking oil, and a man-trap. The heroic ending is a test of his masculinity, a departure for Dustin from his antihero characters.

Hoffman scores another solid award-winning performance as David Sumner, who is a cross between Benjamin Braddock and his romantic screen character, John. Throughout the film, he changes his character—from an intellectual mathematician to a violent demon—at the flick of a switch. The character of David requires as much of the actor in terms of dramatics and pathos as that of Ratso Rizzo.

Susan George proves in many ways why she shines as one of England's most sexual screen vamps. And Sam Peckinpah lives down past critics' comments that in his films violence is carried to an extreme without reason, because in *Straw Dogs,* he defines that reason with good pacing and deliberate direction. Peckinpah and David Z. Goodman deserve laurels also for a coherent job in collaborating on the screenplay adaptation of the Gordon M. Williams novel.

Time magazine extolled the film as "a brilliant feat of movie-making. Hoffman's performance is nervously cerebral and superbly realized. Susan George, all teasing, feline sexuality, carries off a difficult role extremely well. . . . But it is Peckinpah who dominates and controls his material." Not all critics agreed that *Straw Dogs* was a cinematic masterpiece, as *Variety* downgraded the film's script for showing "a weakness in development, shallow characterization, and lack of motivation. . . . The Dustin Hoffman and Sam Peckinpah names can get them into a theater. After that it will be a case of personal taste."

Despite some critics' vocal displeasure over the film's violent climax, Peckinpah's depiction of a real social problem must have hit home with the habitual filmgoers. *Straw Dogs* amassed over $4.5 million in domestic revenue and $3.5 million in foreign box-office grosses, combining for over $8 million in total revenue. Evidently, stealing part of the *Variety* critic's review, filmgoers must have believed Peckinpah and Hoffman made good box-office appeal, prompting many of them to catch the film more than once.

Like his earlier film roles, *Straw Dogs* made more visi-

ble Dustin's strong ability to portray any kind of character. That deserves special mention, since Hoffman was
playing a role that wasn't his normal kind of antihero
screen persona. David was repressed, timid, requiring an
uncustomary restrained approach by Dustin—unlike the
bravura style of acting he had popularized in previous
productions. With a film like *Straw Dogs* to his credit,
Hoffman was exploring his full potential in film-making.
Perhaps subsequent ventures would lead him to the superstardom that until now had been eluding him.

7

Picking and Choosing
Papillon

Unlike other top-bracket film stars, Hoffman had already shown in a comparatively short time his ability to enact a diversity of roles. Never satisfied, he was eager to get started on another film project immediately. Hoffman was now in the position most actors often dreamed about: He was able to be choosy about his roles, and for good reason—he was making a six-figure salary in excess of five hundred thousand dollars per picture, including a percentage of the profits from each.

And Dustin was choosy. He sifted through an avalanche of offers, while his agent continued negotiating a lucrative deal that would make Hoffman a partner in First Artists Productions. Other big-name luminaries had already come to terms as shareholders in the company— Paul Newman, Barbra Streisand, Steve McQueen, and Sidney Poitier.

The formal announcement of Hoffman's signing was made on September 12, 1971, at National General Pictures' international conference for foreign film distributors in Hollywood. The meeting of nearly seventy-five distributors was being held in salute of First Artists Productions, whose distributor was National General Pictures. Part of Dustin's agreement included a salary of over $1 million per film and fifty percent of each film's box-office revenue. As if that wasn't enough, his contract contained a clause granting him the distinct ability to have creative control over his films—even final say on editing.

First Artists was originally formed to attract big box-office stars who were tired of bureaucratic controls at other major studios. The idea was to offer each film star a rich financial package—including creative control. Some of First Artists' principal shareholders, like Sidney Poitier, were already producing films for release at the time of Hoffman's signing. Dustin had been seeking a number of properties, but nothing really appealed to him. Instead, he was intrigued with another film offer waiting in the wings at Paramount Pictures. The actor was being fervently sought for the lead role of a homosexual murderer in a hard-hitting drama, entitled *The Witness*. Milos Forman was directing this mystery-thriller, with Max Setton producing. Unfortunately, what might have been Dustin's most offbeat role didn't materialize, because the film project was scrapped at the last minute.

Dustin's next film offer was undoubtedly one of his best, earning him $1.2 million. In early September, he was cast as costar opposite Steve McQueen in the screen version of Henri Charriere's best-selling novel, *Papillon*.

The film marked the first time Hoffman had the pleasure of working with McQueen, himself a superstar. Allied Artists, which was producing the venture, had complete faith in the box-office combination of McQueen and Hoffman to offset the film's $13 million budget. Confident of success too, Dustin was accompanied by his wife to Jamaica, the ocean island setting for *Papillon* (Anne was signed to guest star in the film). Frank J. Schaffner, who produced and directed the Academy Award-winning screen biography *Patton,* was hired to direct the film and Robert Dorfman was to produce it.

In an interview, Schaffner once remarked that the major problem with *Papillon* was transferring the novel successfully into a screenplay, since the book contained no real human relationships. So in an effort to make the film workable, he decided to create some characters—including Papillon's myopic partner, Louis Dega, whom Hoffman played.

Although Allied Artists was high on the film's prospects, theater managers were seemingly less confident, despite the team of McQueen and Hoffman. Evidently, managers were leery about a $13 million film making back its profit; Allied Artists wasn't so concerned. In the wake of such skepticism, studio president Emanuel L. Wolf said he was confident that McQueen and Hoffman, whom he labeled as "superstars," would lift the film out of the red following its release to theaters. As he said, "If those two [Hoffman and McQueen] don't qualify, I don't know who does."

Dustin has said that the first week of filming in the tropics of Jamaica was "just nerve-wracking." When he takes on a role, he becomes more tense before the movie even starts filming. Hoffman admits that sometimes he becomes so wrapped up with his screen characters that he forgets his true identity.

While making *Papillon,* Dustin lost twenty pounds, not from physical strain but from the emotional demands of the role, although surely, the tropical climate had some effect. But Hoffman was starting to enjoy acting, and film-making in general, less. "All pictures are hard work, although some actors have an easier time than others. There are actors who like making movies, but I've never enjoyed it," Hoffman once confessed. "I've got a calendar from the day I start shooting, and I start crossing off the days the way I did in high school, waiting for summer vacation to begin."

Perhaps, the fact that Dustin's work had yet to receive recognition among his peers as Oscar caliber contributed to these feelings. He was also finding film roles unrewarding in comparison to the joy of the Broadway stage. Another factor might have been the long separations he had to endure from his family. In order to rectify any homesickness, Dustin invited Anne and Karina and Jennifer to stay with him throughout the entire filming schedule of his latest movie. Then, when the roles became more demanding and his own tension began worsening, he cut down on the amount of time his family would spend with him. As he once explained: "Any experience that affects you physically and emotionally will carry over. You can be exhausted after a day's work, depressed. If you're working with anger, opening up your own emotional areas for the film, you go home and carry that anger with you. After leaving work, I have to make a conscious effort to leave those troubles behind."

Hoffman may have also been plain bored with not only film-making but society in general. He said: "Away from work, most films bore me. I'd rather read for entertainment. We live in a period of great passivity, where audiences prefer to sit and look at films, sit and listen to music, sit and watch sports on TV. They don't participate. Art has never been for the masses, but now people seem to see what's good. The least I can do is try to make what I do as artistic as possible."

Known in Hollywood as a difficult actor, Dustin's bitter attitude over film-making and acting comes as no surprise. Generally, his feelings vary widely according to his mood on any given day. Crew members around the set try ignoring his unexpected outbursts, which are usually caused by his creative differences with directors and other actors. For all of those critics of his complex attitude, however, he has issued one word of caution. "They should think twice before they rail against me," Dustin told *Time* magazine correspondent James Willwerth. "They may have done their best work with me. I'm like that clocker who is always saying, 'Come on! Come on! Come on!'"

Filming on the set of *Papillon* was no exception. He started telling his comrades around the set that the role of Louis Dega had become one of his most challenging roles and a personal favorite. Hoffman was likewise enjoying the camaraderie with Steve McQueen, besides the opportunity of working with his wife, Anne, who was making her screen debut as the wife of Louis Dega.

Opening on December 19, 1973, at New York's Sutton Theater, the film received less than glowing raves from critics. Their main criticism concerned the film's length and one-dimensional characters. Critics denounced the script also as being underdeveloped, advising filmgoers to draw their own conclusions. They did: *Papillon* racked up enormous profits during its first week—over $3 million—and $15 million by the second month of release! Although the film was far from a critical standout, at least box-office-wise Dustin was laughing all the way to the bank.

The film's title character, Charriere (nicknamed Papillon because of a butterfly tattoo on his chest), is a convicted pimp murderer sentenced to Devil's Island. While en route by ship to the famous prison in French Guiana, Papillon meets a bespectacled, timid counterfeiter, too weak to protect himself, named Louis Dega (Dustin Hoffman). Their friendship begins with Papillon offering Dega protection in exchange for financing his escape.

The story takes on the theme of "the survival of the fittest," focusing on the cruelty of the prison system, with some heavy dramatic episodes: convicts knifing one another, mutilating themselves to get into the prison hospital, and rushing out on abortive escape attempts. In the meantime, Dega tries helping Papillon fuel his escape (he makes eight unsuccessful escapes until the ninth leads him to freedom). Papillon's successful escape lands him permanent residence in Venezuela, until he is reunited with Dega on a South American coastal island. By the time Papillon gains his freedom, however, he is old and gray, a broken man. Perhaps the most affectionate scene in the film comes when Dega embraces his longtime friend, Papillon, prior to his leap off the island's cliff into the watery depths below.

In this male love story Hoffman gives another resounding performance as the sickly, compassionate Dega, his hair shaven to the bone and sporting wire-rim bifocals. His screen characterization of the meek, pathetic, nearsighted con man left audiences truly sympathetic, notably after the loss of his dearest friend, Papillon.

McQueen likewise shines as the tragic figure of Papillon. On screen, the two actors seem as if they had been working together for years. Although critics were of another opinion, Frank J. Schaffner manages to direct what might be his best picture to date, excluding *Patton.* His frankness and unrestraint on screen helps make the characters of Papillon and Dega seem real, as well as the circumstances that surround them.

Critics were less easily convinced. Judith Crist, in a review in *The New Yorker*, stated that *Papillon* "shows moviegoers that the talents of even Dustin Hoffman and Steve McQueen can be buried under endless restatement of the obvious and the best adventure stories can be attenuated into boredom." *Newsweek* was even more direct when it said: "*Papillon* offers torture as entertainment but winds up as making entertainment a form of torture." *Hollywood Reporter*, catching the film in a different light, said: "Under Schaffner's rigorous control, Hoffman rediscovers the disciplines which has evaded him in recent roles." Even Richard Schickel of *Time* magazine remarked: "McQueen works hard and almost manages to triumph over his star presence, while Hoffman submerges himself eccentrically and amusingly in his coward's role."

Despite the fact that critics were down on the film, Allied Artists was elated over the colossal box-office returns the film was amassing nationwide. So was Hoffman. The film's $3 million gross during its first week was the highest single box-office gross of any film in Allied Artists' forty-six-year history! Dustin was also beaming from ear to ear when he received word of the film's worldwide success—and for obvious reasons: He was taking five percent of the profits from *Papillon*'s first $14 million and twenty-five percent of the picture's first $500,000. Some bargain, eh?

Hoffman may have needed an armored car to haul his earnings off to the bank, since another film he co-produced and starred in nearly two years earlier was finally reaching the screen. *Alfredo, Alfredo* was released nationwide the same day as *Papillon*. Strangely enough, critics were slightly more receptive to this low-budget Italian comedy than they were to an action-adventure film like *Papillon*. Maybe it wasn't so surprising, since one of Italy's most renowned directors, Pietro Germi, was at the helm.

Alfredo, Alfredo was similar to Germi's earlier divorce-oriented romps, with one exception: It starred an American actor in the lead for the first time. Usually his films were loaded with a legion of no-name Italian stars, at least no-names to this country, who had little drawing power in America. Hoffman certainly maintained drawing power; the problem was, what would his fans think of him in an Italian-speaking film? Hoffman and Germi would soon find out.

Alfredo, Alfredo is another comedy with a sexual theme, with Dustin as an ingenuous bank clerk, Alfredo, who falls in love with an undersexed comely pharmacist (Stefanià Sandrelli). Their encounter leads to the marriage bed, leaving Alfredo a mental and physical wreck. His doctor recommends sex three times a day with his wife in order to make her pregnant—and cure her illness. His aggravation is compounded when his wife keeps embarrassing him at the dinner table, delighting herself in sucking fish heads, and in bed, screaming like an air-raid siren during sex.

Dustin, with his hair slicked back and wearing tight pants, soon finds his marriage to this sex-tease pharmacist too much to handle. So he files for divorce, leading him next into the arms of another woman (Carla Gravina) and taking on a similar marriage-go-round when he marries this lively, sexy woman. Alfredo's life thus continues to take a course similar to a never-ending roller-coaster ride, when his estranged wife, the pharmacist, tangles in a legal battle with her ex-husband. Perhaps, the film's underlying message is that marriage and divorce work hand and hand—or that neither is worth the trouble.

Hoffman is brilliant in the lead role, shining in many

wife-husband scenes and in those with his Italian in-laws. Although the film appears to take on a bittersweet feeling about marriage, the Alfredo character manages to lessen the effects of this statement, thanks in large to Dustin's balanced portrayal. It would also seem that Hoffman takes enough bold steps to avoid letting his characterization of Alfredo step beyond the statement Germi's comedy romp maintains. Maybe Germi deserves a round of applause as well for his stable and efficient direction of a common social matter that can oftentimes be touchy.

Germi's dim view of marriage didn't seem to faze critics, either. *Los Angeles Times* critic Charles Champlin remarked that the film "moves swiftly" and pulls off "some zany inventions." Champlin said also that even though Dustin required subtitles, he "suffers nothing in the translation." (Germi, at the last minute, decided to dub Hoffman instead of letting the actor speak in his own native tongue.) Showing equal praise was *Los Angeles Herald-Examiner* critic Richard Cuskelly, who wrote that *Alfredo, Alfredo* was "often amusing in the broad farce style of low Italian humor, and it reminds us of the intricate idiocies the law of marriage can sometimes conjure up to vex us." His only objection was dubbing Dustin with someone else's voice. Cuskelly believed that in this case a voice as recognizable as Hoffman's would be preferred over that of some second-rate Italian actor.

In fact, the primary issue of complaint in most reviews was the dubbing of Hoffman. As *Newsweek* critic Arthur Cooper quipped: "The lips that move are his own, but the sounds they make are the anonymous mutterings of some Italian actor." *Time* magazine spared no biting humor in its remarks: "Robbing an actor of his voice is like chopping off an acrobat's legs. Hoffman remains undaunted, even though watching him is like seeing Jerry Mahoney [a ventriloquist dummy] doing a solo act."

The year 1973 was financially a success, but critically mediocre. *Papillon,* though a box-office sensation, was hardly a critical one, and *Alfredo, Alfredo,* a surprise film of the year, astounded critics in general.

Dustin was to star in yet another production after completion of *Papillon,* but perhaps, his own principles interfered. He was against the idea of making over two films per year, believing an actor should avoid too much exposure. The film offer was for *Friday, the Rabbi Slept Here,* which was to be his first starring film for First Artists and a pilot for a possible series based on Harry Kemelman's rabbi-turned-detective novel series. The property had been originally considered by Twentieth Century-Fox in August 1972, but it was eventually dropped. Later, the property found its way to First Artists, where it was agreed the film would be co-produced with Wanger International Pictures with Ulu Grosbard directing. Somehow the deal collapsed and Dustin was set free to concentrate on other projects.

Actually, Dustin had about as much of the limelight as he wanted for one year, preferring, in typical fashion, to forget the ups and downs of 1973 and concentrate on his future. Hoffman was aware that he couldn't afford another lukewarm picture, but fortunately, his previous films hadn't tarnished his superstar image too badly. Instead, he was confident of emerging with his share of successes in the days ahead.

Hoffman in his off-Broadway days.

Flanked by a Great Dane in a film that was a dog indeed,
Madigan's Millions (1969).

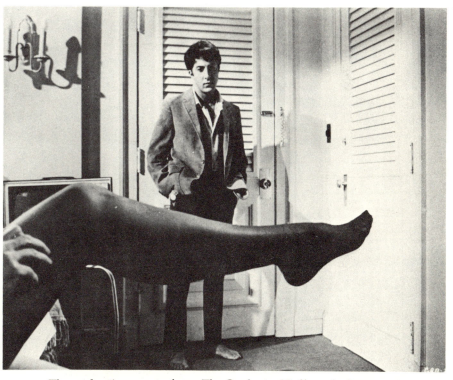

The seduction scene from *The Graduate*, Hoffman's first starring role.

Hoffman strikes a
relaxed pose in
this early portrait.

One of his great performances, as Ratso Rizzo in *Midnight Cowboy* (1968).

With technical crew of Broadway's *Jimmy Shine*: co-producer Claire Nichtern, writer Murray Schisgal, director Donald Driver, and producer Zev Buffman.

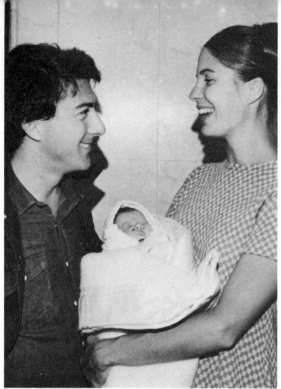

Above, Hoffman and his wife prepare to leave the hospital with the new addition to their family, Jennifer Celia, born on October 15, 1970. *Photograph from Wide World Photos.*

As the comedian Lenny Bruce in the film *Lenny*, which won Hoffman his third Oscar nomination.

Hoffman's third most popular role,
that of Louis Dega in *Papillon*.

With *Washington Post* editors Ben Bradlee and Howard Simons at a cast party for *All the President's Men.*

Wife Anne Byrne congratulates Hoffman on being named Entertainer of the Year in 1975 (*top left*). With Robert Redford off the set of *All the President's Men* (1976) (*left*).

Hoffman and second wife Lisa talking with activist Bella Abzug at a UCLA Women's Week. *Photograph from Jay Alan Samit.*

At the 52nd Annual Academy Awards, Hoffman is flanked by *Kramer vs. Kramer* costar Meryl Streep, director Robert Benton, and producer Stanley R. Jaffe. *Photograph from Long Photography.*

With Justin Henry, who plays his son in *Kramer vs. Kramer*.

Dustin Hoffman as he looks today.

8

The Third Disappointment
Lenny, directing on Broadway

Besides honing his talents as an actor, Dustin was finding that comedy was something that came naturally, perhaps because he was born with the talent for the art of slapstick. Thus it may have come as no revelation when Hoffman was chosen to enact the life of comedian Lenny Bruce in Bob Fosse's film *Lenny*.

Film producer Marvin Worth, Lenny's longtime friend, had been trying to produce a screen biography on the late comedian since 1968, and he eventually sparked the interest of Bob Fosse in producing the film with him. And Fosse's first selection for the role was Dustin. Fosse was a superstar of sorts himself. His credits were sprinkled with an impressive array of honorary feats—two Tony Awards for Broadway's *Pippin*, an Oscar for the movie *Cabaret*, and an Emmy for "Liza with a Z," a TV special starring Liza Minnelli. Dustin likewise had amassed a similar number of honors, so taking on the role of Lenny was like the icing on the cake as far as he was concerned. Fosse was apparently convinced that

Hoffman was *the* best equipped candidate to portray Bruce, since his outward physical appearance visually resembled Bruce's and his acting would definitely register with filmgoers the impression that Lenny Bruce was still alive.

Fosse wasn't as quick in picking an actress to star opposite Hoffman as Bruce's wife, Honey. He spent weeks testing up to thirty women a day with Dustin in love scenes. Hoffman has said that he didn't mind the variety of love scenes, since it gave him a chance to kiss "about ninety of the best-looking girls in town." There were mutterings in and around Hollywood, in the meantime, that actress-singer Joey Heatherton was a shoo-in for the role. Heatherton was voluptuous and the raw, sensuous kind of woman able to tease male filmgoers into spending dollars at the box office.

Much to everyone's amazement, however, Fosse contracted an up-and-coming starlet instead of a veteran. Actress Valerine Perrine, who had been a smash in *Slaughterhouse Five*, was signed to star as Honey, which was okay by Dustin, thank you. Perrine was tailor-made for the role, since she had been a Las Vegas stripper and understood the grounds from which Honey got her start. With the selection of Perrine, Hoffman embarked with the rest of the crew on a sixteen-week filming schedule taking them to Miami, Florida, in January 1974.

Lenny was Hoffman's toughest screen character, perhaps tougher than Ratso Rizzo and Louis Dega combined. He was portraying a world-famous comedian, not a fictional character created purely for the sake of a story. Certainly Dustin wasn't particularly comfortable having to act as a stand-up comedian, let alone Bruce, without ever having known him. Throughout his career, Hoffman has been known to become obsessed with preparing for

his screen roles, much in the same manner as an archae-
ologist on a new site. For Hoffman, performing as Lenny
was an intellectual experiment, because he had to improvise as Bruce, not act like the comedian. Fosse has
recalled in interviews that it was mentally and physically
important that Hoffman convince critics as Lenny, especially in the nightclub scenes, where Dustin reenacted
many of Bruce's most remembered monologues.

To capture Bruce as he actually was, Hoffman spent
three months listening to records, watching films, and
reading books on the comedian. He also interviewed over
sixty people who knew Bruce intimately, in order to relate some small part of Lenny's idiosyncrasies to his own
life. Of those Dustin interviewed, he has credited Bruce's
mother for providing him with the clearest account of
Lenny as a person. Up until that time, Hoffman felt overtly
uncomfortable about portraying Lenny, a person he had
never known.

Even though he started feeling at ease, Dustin has
said that performing the famed comedian's nightclub
monologues were "nervous times" for him and the
toughest obstacle to overcome. Fosse staged these seg-
ments in several Miami nightclubs with a live audience
invited in to watch the proceedings. Hoffman has admitted that he was petrified over performing the material he
was about to reprise with a live audience looking on.
Hoffman started relaxing when Fosse advised him to just
forget about the audience and do his lines. Some of
Fosse's advice, however, quickly resulted in an argument
with Hoffman, who blew his stack before the disagreement was resolved. Fosse once explained in an interview
the reason for the actor's sudden outburst. As he recalled, "Dustin had never done anything like this before.
The audience was making him nervous, so I put the cam-

eras on him, and we rapped back and forth like a television warm-up. It is much easier for performers to become actors. It is more difficult to make an actor become a performer." Hoffman has acknowledged the fact that he is a difficult actor—a reputation he readily admits. "My conduct hasn't changed," he once said. "I've always been known to be hard, to be a perfectionist."

While directing *Lenny*, Fosse was able to explore not only his own theory of turning Dustin from an actor into a performer, but Hoffman's theory of being "a perfectionist" at full-scale. A studio publicist kept denying reports that the director was humiliating the stars of *Lenny*, only admitting that Fosse had an unusual style. That unusual style was resorting to shock tactics in bringing out the kind of emotional reaction he expected from an actor. *Lenny* was just another example.

On several occasions, Hoffman was witness to Fosse using these pressure tactics on Valerine Perrine, his co-star. In one scene, for example, Perrine was supposed to break down and cry. She did but Fosse was dissatisfied with her show of tears, so he told her that her dog had been hurt, which turned her next reaction to one of grief-stricken pain. Then, during another scene, Fosse was filming the reaction of the audience during Hoffman's nightclub performance as Lenny. One of the extras wasn't giving the kind of facial reaction Fosse demanded during the scene, so he scolded the actor before everyone while the cameras were rolling. The shot of the actor slack-jacked in dismay remains in film to this day.

With filming continuing at an almost unbelievably frantic pace, Dustin took a few moments from shooting to explain his own view of the Lenny myth. "I don't believe Lenny used drugs just to get wasted. Instead, I thought he used them to keep himself going for four days, since he was under enormous pressure from performing in clubs, writing new material, recording new record albums, and planning concerts." Dustin observed also that working was as crucial to Lenny's existence as was his material. It was when the work was taken away from him because of drug busts that Lenny began to fall apart. His constant legal battles over his material were also a contributing factor, since he was unable to perform his "lewd material" without fearing another police arrest. Dustin has said that once he studied Lenny he realized that after the legal encounters were over, the comedian's real work was gone. His career, in effect, was ruined and Hoffman believes Bruce knew that as well, thus committing suicide. All of these insights, according to Dustin, enabled him to bring to the screen a true-to-life portrayal of the famous nightclub comedian.

Hoffman's least favorite recollection was of the filming conditions. During one afternoon filming installment, Valerie Perrine and he were to play a love scene in a hotel room under record temperatures of 105 degrees. Dustin has recalled that the incident was just an unforgettable ordeal. As he said, "They had to seal up the room and air conditioning couldn't be used, because it would hurt the sound. Here we were baking and sweating and doing this love scene together, and we couldn't even see straight. I kept wishing that I was back in a studio that was silently air conditioned. Here you couldn't think about anything except the terrific weather conditions."

Unreal weather conditions were the least of the film's problems, however. Hoffman remembers that perhaps the most complicated situation was gaining permission to film courtroom scene battles of himself as Lenny in a Dade County courtroom. Chief Judge Thomas Lee,

Jr., first rejected the request for use of several courtrooms during the weekdays because of a shortage of courtroom space. Dustin has said that Bob Fosse then proposed filming on weekends, but the judge had another bureaucratic excuse: The courts didn't operate on Saturdays and Sundays. Also, Judge Lee wouldn't okay the request because the city would be held liable for any accident that might occur during filming. In a last-ditch effort to gain use of the courtroom, Fosse submitted a final appeal to the courthouse committee, which subsequently reviewed the dialogue of Lenny, ruling it "obscene and improper." Despite such a judicial roadblock, the scene was filmed elsewhere and Hoffman was able to complete his filming in six months before flying back home, with an exhausted film crew aboard.

While *Lenny* was being prepared for its initial theatrical release, Dustin admitted in an interview that he saw the role as the toughest of his career, comparing the task to his tireless efforts in preparing for his earlier favorite roles of Ratso Rizzo and Jack Crabb. But, actually, Hoffman isn't the kind of actor who compares his past performances to other acclaimed works, preferring critics and his fans to judge each performance on its own merits. Yet, comparisons were unavoidable.

Dustin likes to think that in Lenny he brought the extremities of the comedian's character in full focus. He believes also that he saw the film's viewpoint in a different light from others. "The whole point of the movie was that Lenny was a man who loved his country. Lenny believed in the Constitution, in the right of freedom of speech. He didn't use those four-letter words to make the audience horny; he was just saying, 'Why can't we use the language on stage that we use in our daily lives?'"

Nobody seemed to have that answer, not even Hoffman, or Lenny Bruce might still be alive today, and it's the reason *Lenny* ends with that question unresolved.

Although Lenny was truly a screen character Hoffman thrived on, he had to pass up many other important screen roles as a result. He was offered Jack Nicholson's role in *Five Easy Pieces* and that of Michael in *The Godfather* (which went to Al Pacino). Both roles would have been extraordinary additions to his already broad range of screen portrayals.

Yet, Dustin was delighted with his career so far and was in no rush to push himself into any role that came along. One that would have fallen into this category was that of Jesus Christ in Franco Zeffirelli's $12 million television epic, "The Life of Jesus," which Hoffman wisely turned down. Zeffirelli also started experiencing second thoughts himself, later remarking, "How do you convince an audience that he [Dustin] is Christ?" Yes, that would have been difficult all right. Another factor was Hoffman's reluctance to portray the life of another historical figure so soon after *Lenny*.

Lenny was a blockbusting critical and financial success when it opened November 8, 1974. Business was as torrential as a hurricane, tearing up box-office records the first day at Manhattan's Cinema I. The film not only amassed over $14,918 on opening day, but kept racking up the same kind of impressive figures in weeks to come. *Lenny*, in fact, kept doing stunning business in New York, long before the film was even released nationwide one month later.

Lenny is a penetrating, surreal portrayal of the late nightclub comedian. The complexities of Bruce's character emerge in flashback form, interspersed with interviews with those who knew Lenny. His former wife, Honey (Valerie Perrine), starts off the film with her remembrances of Bruce doing impersonations of both Jimmy Durante and singer Morgan White in his nightclub act. At first glimpse, his comedy doesn't seem to exceed that of the average nightclub stand-up—in fact, it fails miserably at first. Then, Lenny begins changing into a demonic character, out to cure the world's social and po-litical problems, using four-letter words in his nightclub monologue.

The human side of Lenny's real-life character is soon revealed following a tasteless nightclub engagement in a Las Vegas-style showroom featuring Sherman Hart (Gary Morton) as the master of ceremonies. Known as "Mr. En-tertainment" (patterned after Milton Berle), Hart advises Bruce to abandon using offensive language in his act if he plans on surviving in show business. The survivor that Lenny is, he walks onstage and starts apologizing to the audience for a dirty remark he made the night before, only to change his tune, adding, "So I would like to piss on you all." Bruce is, needless to say, kicked off the nightclub bill and kicked out of the club by the manager, and warned again that he will never make it in show business with his kind of act.

Tragedy soon intercedes as Lenny's life starts taking a downhill spin: He mixes with drugs; he has affairs with other women; he refuses to clean up his foul language in nightclubs despite constant surveillance by police and legal entanglements; and ultimately, Bruce dies of a drug overdose.

Hoffman makes filmgoers laugh, cry, and empathize with a man caught in a backward society—backward in the sense that his comedy was too advanced for its time.

Bruce's style of controversial humor is crisply reenacted by Dustin, who definitely comes off as a performer rather than as an actor. He successfully manages to make audiences believe, for at least a good portion of the movie, that he *is* Lenny Bruce and not Dustin Hoffman. Like Bruce, Hoffman is real, sensitive, demanding, crude, and offensive.

Valerie Perrine is tantalizing as Bruce's seductive wife, Honey. Her greatest moments are her love scenes and those as a Las Vegas stripper, the latter carried off rather tastefully. Gary Morton is a delight as Sherman Hart, and Jan Miner does a vivid characterization of Bruce's overprotective mother. Bob Fosse, through his on-target direction, shows his knack for making the tragic biography of Lenny Bruce believable, powerful, and timeless.

Lenny won the acceptance not only of movie fans but of critics also. They regarded the epic as a unique lesson of one of our country's "precursors of social upheaval . . . and like most pioneers he got clobbered for his foresight." Fosse's direction was often compared to that of Orson Welles's in *Citizen Kane,* since he used the unseen reporter as the glue that holds the story together.

Most of all, however, critics gave Dustin nothing but raves for his performance. *Variety* appraised his portrayal of Lenny as "another outstanding performance." *Hollywood Reporter,* whose remarks were similar, stated that the film "could well boast that Dustin Hoffman *is* Lenny, for his performance is unique and compelling." Even picky *Time* magazine critic Richard Schickel lauded Hoffman for "giving a complex and mercurial performance. . . . His mimicry of Bruce's onstage mannerisms is uncanny, but what is awesome is the range of emotion he commands in the intimate scenes." Hoffman had given Hollywood and the world a masterful performance that seemed unmatched by his previous film efforts.

By March 1975, just five months after its release, *Lenny* had already grossed $11,499,096 from engagements in 316 theaters. United Artists, the film's producing company, reported that among the largest single city grossers were: New York, $2,427,000; Los Angeles, $1,375,500; Philadelphia, $738,264; Detroit, $576,500; San Francisco, $569,900; and Canada, $727,200.

Despite the astronomical success of *Lenny*, a real tragedy struck prior to the release of the film that marred the festivities. Director Bob Fosse was hospitalized in a New York hospital for a severe coronary condition on October 30, 1975. He was operated on several days later for a blocked artery near his heart and was immobilized in the hospital for four weeks. Fosse never did get a chance to celebrate the completion of *Lenny*. But that didn't stop Hoffman from trying to cheer up his ill director. Dustin had a gorgeous flower arrangement delivered to Fosse's room and also kept in touch by phone. It was also around this time that Dustin spoke of the director in an interview: "Fosse's a very fair man. He's a very hard-working director, and there are some things he doesn't tolerate. He drives himself to death literally. He doesn't tolerate it when a person doesn't do his job. He's not only someone who's gifted but someone who works hard."

Dustin was thankful that the director selected him to portray Lenny, even though he had been given less than a year to prepare. Although he liked Fosse as a director, Hoffman has said that during production of *Lenny* he argued over certain aspects of the character and compromised with Fosse. He pointed out that there was a lot of give-and-take with the director and writer, although he felt strongly about his point of view. Dustin personally feels that the film is "a flawed work, and certainly not Lenny Bruce," an opinion that might prompt some surprise from fans and critics.

Hoffman doesn't consider *Lenny* a dishonest account, nor exploitative, but has gone on record saying that filmgoers don't "get to know enough" about Lenny, even though he believes what was shown is valid and accurate. Dustin's feelings indicate he is never satisfied with his work, always analyzing, always breaking down his strengths and weaknesses, always feeling he can do better.

Dustin's versatility as an actor doesn't end here. One month before *Lenny* was released, Hoffman began his first assignment as a director of his first Broadway stage production since he assisted Ulu Grosbard in 1964. The stage revue, *All Over Town*, was a comedy written by Murray Schisgal (who ten years earlier had gained prominence for his contemporary comedy, *Luv*, and remains one of Dustin's closest friends offstage).

About the same time, newspaper reporters were circulating rumors around New York that Hoffman was divorcing his wife, Anne, and that he was living in an Oakland commune with an art student named Patty, who was allegedly engaged to the actor. Anne didn't want to believe the story, and Hoffman said the entire incident was someone's tasteless concoction and held not one ounce of truth. Shaking his head in disbelief when confronted with the story, Dustin said, "Why the night before I even got a call from a man who said he was going to be my father-in-law. I started wondering what my wife was thinking of me."

Even though Hoffman tried ignoring this kind of

sensationalist reporting, the story had accurately pin-pointed another Hoffman trait: He's a womanizer. Meryl Streep, who later costarred with Dustin in *Kramer vs. Kramer*, remembers her first audition of *All Over Town* as unpleasant, saying in an interview: "He [Hoffman] came up to me and said, 'I'm Dustin—burp—Hoffman,' and he put his hand on my breast. 'What an obnoxious pig,' I thought." Even Dustin has admitted on occasion that he loves to flirt, claiming that he does it as an involuntary reflex. He has supposedly cornered women in elevators to solicit sex and has even unzipped one woman re-porter's blouse to peek down her chest during an inter-view. He tries to catch himself, but finds it difficult to overcome the temptation.

Although Dustin's interest in other women some-times surfaces during work, he was finding that produc-ing *All Over Town* was creating enough problems on its own. When *All Over Town* was first written, seven Broad-way producers expressed fervent interest in backing the stage play—but then all of them lost interest, suddenly, leaving Hoffman not only discouraged but without a producer.

Determined to succeed, Dustin got a list of potential backers from the Kennedy Center in Washington, only to be turned down by each and every one. He was able to scrounge up $100,000 from film producer Joseph E. Le-vine, but Dustin later described the process of searching out backers like "being at a crap table." The more calls he made, the more discouraged he became.

The last backer he reached was Adela Holzer, who had financed the Broadway musical *Hair*. She reluctantly agreed to produce *All Over Town*, which naturally elated Dustin. A short time later, however, Hoffman became embroiled in a disagreement with Levine, his smallest backer, who angrily withdrew his money. That left Dustin still short of cash: He had to raise at least a half a million dollars. The situation started growing grimmer, so Dustin and his good friend Gene Hackman scraped up the remaining funds—a figure estimated at over $300,000—out of their own pockets to get the show off the ground.

Dustin has said that financing the show was the least of his worries. It had over sixteen major characters, more than any stage production in modern times. Murray Schisgal and Hoffman spent weekends auditioning over fifteen hundred actors, not all of them professionals— cabdrivers, janitors, and shoeshine men—but not all of them talented either. Finalists chosen to headline the show were Cleavon Little as the clever opportunist (a role that Schisgal says was originally created for Little), Barnard Hughes as an absentminded psychiatrist, and Zane Lasky as an oversexed ladies' man. Besides the three main characters, eighteen characters of diverse and ethnic backgrounds also starred in this contemporary comedy about city life. (Dustin has admitted that the next time he directs a Broadway show, it won't involve so many characters.)

At least *All Over Town* gave Dustin a rare opportunity to apply his knowledge as an actor toward directing. He had a style that he had undoubtedly picked up from working with some of Hollywood's enigmatic directors: Ulu Grosbard, a longtime friend, Mike Nichols (who directed *The Graduate*), and Bob Fosse, who became a major influence on him. Hoffman had spent several memorable nights watching Fosse direct his Broadway musical extravaganza, *Pippin*.

Some actors, Hoffman discovered, feel threatened when he runs through scenes first because they have their own way of doing it. That part of working with actors has been something Dustin rarely considers a problem. He believes that understanding actors is one of the first functions of a director, before making suggestions as to how specific scenes or characters should be played. In a number of interviews, Hoffman has likened directing the actors in *All Over Town* to "guiding children."

His months of preparation over, *All Over Town* finally opened for the theater world in Chicago at the Shubert Theatre on Tuesday, August 19, 1975. The show received some chilly reviews its first week in Chicago, before undergoing what Dustin has termed "emergency repairs." When the show resumed its run after these repairs, *All Over Town* showed vast improvements. *Time* magazine, in reviewing the actor's debut as a director, wrote: "Moving 18 actors with the agility of an Osterizer, Hoffman proves that he is only a laugh-beat away from the comedic ingenuity of Mike Nichols." Here it was eight years after Dustin first worked with Nichols on *The Graduate,* and critics were comparing his deft style of direction to that of his former mentor. Dustin actually considered that quite a compliment. In contrast, *Hollywood Reporter* said: "*All Over Town* is overloaded with such comedy ballast as mistaken identity (which is key to the play's working) so that it never really soars. It has been directed by Dustin Hoffman (his first effort at piloting a theatrical vehicle) and while it won't win any prizes, it has enough laughs to win the approval of not-too-demanding audiences. . . . Hoffman's direction might have profited by being a little firmer."

Dustin, however, viewed directing *All Over Town* as "a live-and-learn experience." As he once said: "I did find things I didn't like about the experience: having to work with so many actors. Next time I would prefer a half-dozen actors who were really together. The way Broadway is set up, an actor can't think of it as just a job. Everyone has to work more hours than in a day to make it"—something that Hoffman was certainly willing to do if necessary. In the future, he would also hope to avoid the frustrating experience of thumbing through local telephone directories for producers.

At least, despite the mixed reviews of *All Over Town*, Dustin did receive some enlightening news one bright and early afternoon in March 1975. The Academy of Motion Picture Arts and Science informed him that he had been selected as an Oscar nominee for best actor for his performance in *Lenny*, his third such nomination. In addition, the film was nominated for best director, best actress, best picture, and best screenplay. Hoffman was competing with such stalwarts of the cinema as Art Carney for his outstanding performance in *Harry and Tonto;* Albert Finney for *Murder on the Orient Express;* Jack Nicholson for *Chinatown;* and Al Pacino for his portrayal of Michael in *The Godfather, II.*

But Dustin and the film biography went down to a stunning defeat in all five categories that evening. *The Godfather, II* unanimously took best picture and best director. Art Carney, a man as versatile as Hoffman, grabbed an Oscar for best actor for his performance in *Harry and Tonto.* Valerie Perrine, who was nominated for best actress as the sensual Honey, was nudged out by Ellen Burstyn's compelling performance in *Alice Doesn't Live Here Anymore.* And soundly beating Julian Barry (*Lenny*) for best screenplay was—who else?—Francis Ford Coppola and Mario Puzo (*The Godfather, II).*

The loss was a sour defeat not only for Hoffman, but also for Bob Fosse. Perhaps Dustin was just jinxed when it came to these Academy Award ceremonies—since he had been nominated twice before for best actor and lost. Maybe, the deck of rich talent was too well stacked against him this time. Whatever the reason, Hoffman didn't like thinking about why he had lost. What he wanted above all was for his performance to be remembered.

9

Another Key Performance
All the President's Men

Despite his failure at the Academy Awards, *Lenny* had renewed Hoffman's faith in the film industry's ability to turn out quality motion pictures, ones with the coherent scriptwriting and richly defined characters he needed. Hoffman was now among the top five heavyweight box-office stars in America, along with John Wayne, Burt Reynolds, Robert Redford, and Paul Newman. His role of Lenny had been pivotal in establishing him as a performer and not just as a great character actor.

The same year that *Lenny* was produced, Americans were paying close attention to Watergate, a scandal that was keeping citizens spellbound and was stripping them of their trust in our nation's government. The incident led to court indictments of President Nixon's top aides and the toppling of his administration because of two *Washington Post* reporters, Bob Woodward and Carl Bernstein, who broke the case wide open with a series of investigative articles. Watergate not only became the subject of a best-selling book, *All the President's Men*, but was also adapted into what has become a revolutionary film docudrama starring Robert Redford and Dustin Hoffman as the famed reporters.

Hoffman's interest in the project surfaced following publication of Woodward and Bernstein's book. He became so interested, in fact, that he offered nearly $450,000 to acquire film rights for the book from the *Washington Post* tandem, but another film superstar beat him to the punch: Robert Redford. In an attempt to mend any hard feelings, Redford called Dustin to ask him to star as Bernstein in the film version for Warner Bros. Hoffman was said to have replied, "I thought you'd never ask." Redford was producing the film along with Walter Coblenz under the banner of Redford's production company, Wildwood Enterprises.

With Hoffman costarring, Redford's main concern was finding a director who would give *All the President's Men* a sympathetic vision. In Redford's opinion, the man was Alan J. Pakula, who had last directed the Oscar-winning film *Klute*. Dustin was also anxious to work with Pakula, so it looked as if Hoffman's dream of advancing his career was about to come true. It was also during production of *All the President's Men* that he made the acquaintance of another important Hollywood technician of the art who would later become a fixture in his career. William Goldman, who later wrote Dustin's role for *Marathon Man*, was assigned to pen the screenplay, with Redford assisting.

Although he knew some of newspaper reporters' basic duties, Hoffman was surprised to learn exactly what kind of long and difficult hours reporters must put in to meet deadlines for the daily edition. So, in order to provide himself with enough background material, Dustin studied under Carl Bernstein, spending months watching the process of news-gathering from the ground-floor room at the *Washington Post*. The details involved in publishing a daily newspaper were mind-boggling, to say the least, as Hoffman found out: "I couldn't get over the fact that the paper really does get out every day. Except for a few flurries of activity, it's as quiet as an insurance company. But it's also the *pleasantest* environment I've ever spent any time in."

Dustin soon understood the rigors of newspaper reporting and the consequences involved in publishing a story. Likewise, Redford was careful in studying for his characterization of Bob Woodward. Both planned to play their real-life characters not verbatim but rather as close as necessary to give the audience a feeling for the two reporters.

Since *All the President's Men* covered so many historical aspects of Watergate, it was necessary to use actual locations in Washington, D.C., as well as re-create sets and the personal effects of Woodward and Bernstein. Even the smallest details received special attention. For instance, Warner Bros. erected a set resembling the *Washington Post* office; several tons of trash were carted across the country—for the sake of authenticity—for this newsroom setting; and the phone number of Woodward's telephone was the same in the film as it had been in 1972.

Similar care was also taken in selecting the cast. Jason Robards was picked to star as the *Post*'s gruff executive editor Benjamin C. Bradlee, with Jack Warden as the hard-nosed Harry Rosenberg, the paper's metropolitan editor, and Martin Balsam as Howard Simons, managing editor. Former President Nixon was also to be shown in actual newsreel footage recorded at the time of Watergate, and even the real names of Nixon's aides would be used, since they were public figures.

The cavernous replica of the *Washington Post*'s newsroom was unveiled at the Burbank Studios on July 2,
1975, with Hoffman and Redford present as hosts. At a
cost of $450,000, the newsroom took up two stages com-
bined. The press event was attended by over one hundred journalists (some who were actually fans wanting to
catch a glimpse of Hoffman and Redford) and photogra-
phers ranging from Stan Tretick, the Kennedys' official
photographer, to a man with a 1948 Brownie camera.
Redford was literally drowned in a sea of people, and
Hoffman fared no better. Fleeing an overzealous fan, he
took the reporters through the 33,000-square-foot identi-
cal model of the real *Post* newsroom.

Despite the ruckus, Hoffman managed to squeeze in
his opinion of the film's perspective. "The movie doesn't
have so much to do with what Watergate was, as with
what it represents symbolically. I just resist the symbol of
the picture of Watergate because it's more about the
newspaper business and how it functions and how it op-
erates." On Hoffman, Redford added: "He's a fantastic
actor. Working with him is like working with a stream of
pure electricity. He's so intense and fluid, you can't help
but react."

A few days later, Dustin found himself in the middle
of another chaotic situation, perhaps more damaging to
his image in Hollywood than any incident during his career. Hoffman lambasted the Oscar awards ceremonies
publicly as "ugly and grotesque." His criticisms were first
broadcast during an interview with critic David Sheehan
over the CBS television network. Dustin charged that
politics was a demeaning factor in the annual Academy
Awards sweepstakes, comparing the events to the as-
sassination of Martin Luther King, Jr.

His reference to King related to the postponement of

the 1968 Oscar awards show when over 160 nominees had urged that the show be delayed out of respect for the slain civil rights leader, killed that day. What upset Hoffman was that when the awards show finally aired one month later, "I went out there and Bob Hope was master of ceremonies, and he was making jokes about the postponement and never said a word about Martin Luther King. That's what I found ugly and grotesque. After that, I said I didn't want to come anymore. It was as simple as that."

In addition, Dustin ticked off a list of grievances over the amount of politics apparent in selecting the Oscar winners, saying that the Academy didn't try fulfilling the purpose for which it was established. Dustin pointed out that the Academy was originally formed to award those in the industry whose work was exciting—whether they were electricians, makeup artists, directors, or actors. In other words, he felt that the award was founded under the platform that its annual show was the industry's way of saying "thanks for a job well done."

Dustin was also bugged by the fact that the Oscars' showdown had turned into a contest instead of an honor. He still remembered when John Wayne had stolen the Oscar for best actor from Jon Voight and him for their performances in *Midnight Cowboy*. Dustin realizes now that Wayne's victory was granted more out of respect for the actor than in salute of his performance, and believes also that since then the Academy Awards' board of directors have truly lost sight of the Oscar's true meaning.

The ramifications of his statement surely didn't help his reputation any. But Hoffman felt his opinion was that of the majority in Hollywood, themselves victims of the Academy Awards' politics once too often. Although some people in the industry attacked Dustin for being out of line, Hoffman saw no reason to apologize. Nor did he let the situation interfere with his filming of *All the President's Men*, which was completed in ninety-six days. Due to his embittered feelings with the Academy Awards show and tired from the completion of *All the President's Men*, Dustin knew it was time for a vacation, so he took Anne with him on a short trip to Florida.

Dustin still had ahead of him some paramount decisions. He had a burning desire to return to Broadway, even though he was unable to settle on a worthwhile property. A number of other offers also whetted his appetite, but none were tasty enough to spur his interest.

Two of his next film offer decisions were exactly what Dustin had feared—film biographies of real-life characters. The first script was submitted to Hoffman's agent by former United Artists president David V. Picker, now a producer, who had been impressed by Dustin's performance in *Midnight Cowboy*. Picker was trying to interest Hoffman in playing a flamboyant wrestler modeled after Gorgeous George (a popular wrestler in the fifties) for an untitled film. Dustin turned down the offer. His second major offer was the starring role in a screen biography of former bank robber Willie Sutton, whose autobiography, *Where the Money Was*, was being adapted into a film. Producers Brud Talbot and Ernest Greenberg of Dana-FDM Productions wanted Hoffman, but Dustin rejected the offer flat-out.

Instead, unable to make a career decision so soon, Dustin concentrated on other pressing matters. *All the President's Men* was nearing its theatrical release and Hoffman was getting nervous over how the movie would be received. The American consensus to forget Watergate clouded the film's financial prospects.

The pressure began to mount until *All the President's*

Men premiered at the Loews Astor Plaza in New York on April 8, 1976. Warner Bros. released the film to over five hundred theaters nationwide, grossing over $7 million in seven days, or an average of $1 million per day. *All the President's Men* was not only a gigantic money-maker, but to Dustin's great pleasure, a critical success. Critics unanimously agreed that Redford and Hoffman *were* Woodward and Bernstein in what they termed "a must-see film."

The film opens with the Watergate burglars trying to crack open a safe in the office of the Democratic National Committee located in the Watergate Hotel. Their efforts to undermine the Democrats, since it is during a presidential election year, are revealed when the five men are arrested and brought before a judicial hearing. From here on out, two dogged reporters—Bob Woodward, a cub reporter, and Carl Bernstein, the *Post*'s political reporter—are faced with the difficult task of unearthing details behind the scandal leading to the cover-up by the Nixon administration.

In a day-to-day account of this news-making event, Woodward and Bernstein go to great lengths in digging up material to solve the case. One of the funniest scenes is when this tandem tries nailing Howard Hunt, Nixon's security adviser, for his involvement in the scandal by reviewing what books he checked out from the Library of Congress. Even though the material is ruled confidential, Woodward and Bernstein manage to sneak out several dozen trays of every library request form Hunt submitted to the library during 1971. They flip through literally thousands of forms to sniff out that one vital piece of incriminating information, only to come up empty-handed.

Through a series of newspaper stories, all under the

supervision of their avuncular executive editor, Ben Bradlee (Jason Robards), Woodward and Bernstein start thaw-
ing the ice sealing the Watergate case. Bernstein flies out
to Miami to link a political contributor, Kenneth H.
Dahlberg, to a contribution of over $25,000 to the bank
account of one of the Watergate burglars. Woodward,
meanwhile, hooks up with an unnamed source for information on the Watergate case. The man goes under the
moniker of Deep Throat. Bernstein then manages to
break the silence of a woman bookkeeper who worked
for the CREEP (Committee to Reelect the President,
which was involved in expending money to hire the Watergate burglars). She names the men in Nixon's cabinet
caught up in the cover-up. Then, the final crushing political blow to Nixon and his men is Woodward and Bernstein's exposé that former Attorney General John Mitchell
had acted as the Watergate ringleader. The story leads to
the prosecution of all five of Nixon's men and to the President's eventual resignation.

Hoffman, wearing his hair shoulder-length, adds wit
and charm to what otherwise might have been a rather
dull character. His constant questioning of informants on
Watergate reminds audiences of the dogged way in
which reporters work, and is likewise on-target in depict-
ing the process of news-gathering inside the *Washington
Post*. Dustin's role of Bernstein also casts him in his first
heroic character since *Straw Dogs* and *Madigan's Millions*.

Dustin's stunning performance enhances that of
Robert Redford's as Bob Woodward, his partner. In a surprise move, Redford gave Hoffman top billing in the film,
which he actually deserved, since his character was on
the screen most of the time—and practically stole the
show, according to critics. Jane Alexander is excellent as
the tight-lipped bookkeeper, and Jack Warden is con-

vincing as Harry Rosenberg. Robert Walden, known to American television audiences as Rossi on "Lou Grant," gives an emotional performance as the young, corrupted Nixon attorney Donald Segretti, as does Stephen Collins as Hugh Sloan, Jr. Alan J. Pakula shows great restraint in not directing the film with too much overdramatics—keeping the story more factual and less fictional through his occasional uses of newsreel footage.

Vincent Canby, resident critic for *The New York Times*, enthused: "Mr. Redford and Mr. Hoffman play their roles with a low-keyed understated efficiency required since they are, in effect, the straight men to the people and the events they are pursuing." *New York Post* critic Frank Post added: "This film is a rare and classic example of what Hollywood can do when it's willing to bank good taste, shrewd intelligence and deep personal conviction. Though not perfect, *All the President's Men* is an absolutely breathless entertainment, and successfully carries the weight of history on its shoulders. . . ." As enthusiastic was a reviewer for *Daily Variety*, a Hollywood trade paper, who writes that "Redford and Hoffman excel in their roles as newspaper reporters." Even veteran critic Rex Reed, one of the hardest critics to please in America, remarked: ". . . somehow they [Hoffman and Redford] manage the impossible task of submerging their own superstar images to literally become the reporters they are playing . . . . As different as they are, they merge into one molecular structure in a powerful scene that gave me goose bumps."

The film gave Warner Bros.' executives goose bumps of a different sort when excitement continued to build over the tidy nest egg of revenue the film had already generated: $30 million in less than six months! The movie was being dubbed "a thinking man's *Jaws*." It was good news for Redford, since his company had sunk over $8 million in the film, and also for Hoffman: It was his second smash hit in a row. *Lenny* had commanded remarkable box-office business for a film biography, but *All the President's Men* left no room for comparisons. It wasn't that *Lenny* lacked substance, it was just that the story of the comedian wasn't as controversial and as well-publicized.

The only complaint to surface in critics' reviews was concerning the film's semi-documentary style. Hoffman has agreed with that assertion. As he said, "I told Bob [Redford] that he was drying the picture out. I said he should add a scene where Woodward and Bernstein were really having it out. But he didn't. I would have fought more, but by the time I saw the film, it was too late to make the radical changes I wanted. In my opinion, the film is a little too smooth. I would have left a few hairs on the lens. Instead, the film is really a landmark inasmuch as it's the first movie that really said anything even half-assedly true about the press. Bob deserves this success. Not to take anything away from Alan Pakula, who directed it, but this was Redford's project all the way. He may be the hardest working actor I've ever known."

That year when the the annual Academy Awards ceremonies rolled around, *All the President's Men* was nominated seven times, including for best picture, best director, and best supporting actor. Neither Redford nor Hoffman, despite powerful performances, were nominated. The only people from *All the President's Men* to receive Oscars were Jason Robards for best supporting actor and William Goldman for best screenplay. The implication was that the Academy Awards' board of directors didn't want to support a film containing political overtones. Dustin was undoubtedly overlooked because of his vicious criticisms of the Academy Awards earlier in the year. The National Board of Review must also have found the film's subject too controversial, since it only nominated *All the President's Men* for best picture of the year and honored Jason Robards for best supporting actor. The film won also in these same two categories at the National Society of Film Critics' annual awards banquet.

What to do for an encore? Dustin, never without words, seemed to have an answer: "A success like this always makes me keen to work. So I'll just start looking harder for another good script and hope for the best." Hoffman, it would seem, didn't have to look far, since his performance in *All the President's Men* was enough to whet any producer's appetite.

10

The First Artists Years

Marathon Man, Straight Time, Agatha

With *All the President's Men* setting box-office records, Dustin was now averaging nearly two films per year, which to some of his fans was not enough. Actually, Hoffman was concerned about the longevity of his career. That's why he precludes commercial endorsements or making regular television appearances, as Woody Allen does: to avoid a career burn-out.

Superstar images are terribly difficult to uphold unless that person knows when to adjust his appearances and commitments so he is not in the public's eye too often. As long as he continues putting such safeguards on his career, Dustin is certain to remain one of America's top drawing powers.

His next film and thirteenth of his career, *Marathon Man*, provided the actor with another chance to enhance his superstar image. The film was based on William Goldman's best-selling novel and screenplay, which Robert Evans and Sidney Beckerman were co-producing for Paramount Pictures. Oscar-winning director John Schlesinger, who last piloted Hoffman in *Midnight Cowboy*, was directing, with Sir Laurence Olivier in a costarring role. The film was set in New York and Paris, with a majority of the footage being shot in Manhattan.

Marathon Man wasn't the only film project Hoffman had been considering as a follow-up to his role as Carl Bernstein in *All the President's Men*. Producer Ralph Serpe cornered the actor one afternoon and offered him the starring role in his *Great Brink's Robbery* comedy, featuring an all-star cast of James Caan and Robert Duvall. Serpe asked Hoffman to score the lead role as the gang's leader, with Hal Ashby directing. Dustin changed his mind after reviewing the number of other commitments he had already: two projects he was developing for First Artists and, currently, *Marathon Man*.

The part in Schlesinger's film called for a marathon runner. Dustin was just the actor Paramount was looking for: His specialty in high school had been long-distance running on the school's track team. His lead in *Marathon Man* marked the first time he was starring in a film released under the Paramount Pictures' banner since his ill-fated Italian comedy, *Alfredo, Alfredo.* A film of greater dramatic potential, *Marathon Man* also gave Dustin the opportunity for as intense a portrayal as those in *Straw Dogs* and *Papillon*, as well as another chance to work with Schlesinger, who considered Dustin one of his favorite actors, next to Jack Lemmon. Only this time, Dustin was *the* star. Schlesinger was likewise confident, coming off what critics consider his best film, *Day of the Locust*.

Dustin found working with the English director a distinct pleasure, since he had an affinity for Schlesinger's viewpoint. Schlesinger also knew the merits of making good use of his actors and "getting the most out of them," Hoffman has said. Dustin soon discovered that his role of a New York college student was that special kind of behind-the-makeup role he considered his specialty: not fabricated and less lifelike. Sparing no detail, Hoffman turned to his standard obsession of creating the essential mannerisms and nuances of his characters. Schlesinger gave him very little advice on how he should play the character, although they did have their share of artistic differences over other aspects of the production.

The task of filming *Marathon Man,* at a cost of $3 million, was swiftly completed, and the film's world premiere took place on October 8, 1976, at Mann's Chinese Theater in Hollywood. Hoffman's gigantic legion of fans turned out for the occasion again, expecting a movie equal to *All the President's Men.* Dustin's own self-satisfaction and enthusiasm may have been slightly dimmed, however, when critics thrashed the film as "the disappointment of the year." And news of box-office returns were just as discouraging.

Marathon Man is a largely disjointed espionage affair that fails to live up to its expectations. In the role of Babe Levy, a Columbia University graduate student who is the son of a distinguished historian, Dustin practices daily for the marathon, never knowing that it might save his life.

His main purpose in life and in the film becomes lost in the shuffle of many unattached goings-on, however. Suddenly, one evening, his brother Doc (Roy Scheider) comes stumbling into his apartment, dying in his brother's arms from a knife wound. No explanation is given for his death, other than that an ex-German concentration-camp officer, Christian Szell (Laurence Olivier), has emigrated to America to smuggle out some diamonds belonging to him. Following the death of his brother, Babe is abducted into the hands of Szell who starts performing a brutal, unorthodox root-canal procedure on Levy. Szell tries prying out of him any information his brother may have told him, which he does not possess. Probably the most grotesque scene in the film is watching Hoffman writhe in pain as a result of Szell's impromptu root-canal operation.

Levy is rescued, however, by Janeway (William Devane), a friend of his brother's, who either works for the CIA, FBI, or for Szell; it is never explained. When Levy falls into the ruthless hands of Szell again, he puts his marathon running into practice by escaping from the feared German leader. He is reunited with a mysterious girl friend, Elsa (Marthe Keller), whom he first met while attending Columbia University. She is killed in the aftermath of a gun battle, while Levy tries standing off against Szell. Szell weakens and orders Levy to come out. It turns out that Szell is working for himself—with his own interests at heart—and feels Levy put up such a game fight that he asks him to consider working overseas as a spy.

Hoffman displays a cunning performance as the innocent Babe Levy, showing his ability to perform as a tragic antihero survivor. The film's major fault is basically a complex plot and an uncertain story line. Dustin tried his best under his power to help steer the jumbled film plot in some solvable direction, but to no avail. Schlesinger's incongruous direction contributes to most of the film's inherent problems. Sir Laurence Olivier, who came out of semi-retirement, satisfies in a commanding royal performance as the snide, dastardly Nazi spy. William Devane and Roy Scheider also enhance the film's subpar script with vivid performances.

Despite the film's apparent weaknesses, theater owners reported that business was brisk for the first couple of days, but that after word of mouth got out business started to drop. Critics were labeling the film "a disjointed jigsaw puzzle, minus all the pieces."

Critic Arthur Knight, a veteran movie columnist, was one who came out in support of *Marathon Man*. He perceived the film as "a brilliant and disturbing" movie that provided the audience with "no immediate surface explanations," until the end. Above all, Knight saw that the film contained "a consistency of style and purpose that permits no single performance to stand out (even though the greatest demands are made on Hoffman), nor any of the technical credits to require a special accolade. *Marathon Man* is superior movie-making, period." Just as receptive was *Time* magazine critic Jay Cocks, who wrote: "No doubt *Marathon Man* is the year's most cunning entertainment, a thriller full of spills and shooting, double-dealings, and triple betrayals. It is lavishly mounted and loaded with flash. The movie also offers Dustin Hoffman, giving one of his best performances, up against Laurence Olivier, who is in fine form playing an arch-villain." Cocks also cited director John Schlesinger for bringing out some excellent devices in creating intense drama, including a shell-shocked Hoffman being drowned in his own bathtub by two highly effective agents. Yet, Knight and Cocks seemed to be the only critics who felt *Marathon Man* made any kind of sense whatsoever, while a vast majority of other critics felt the film was missing too many essential ingredients. (*Marathon Man* drew only $8 million, ranking twentieth among the top-grossing films of 1976.)

Returning to his Greenwich Village home and spending time with his family, Dustin tried putting the troubles of *Marathon Man* in the past. He put his energies toward finishing work on a screenplay he planned on starring in and directing. The film was *Straight Time*, which was based on Edward Bunker's novel *No Beast So Fierce* (Bunker was actually an ex-convict), and it was slated to go into production February 9, 1977. Hoffman had bought film rights to the book in 1972 when he had first signed a contract to star in and produce for First Artists Productions.

The movie was to mark Dustin's directorial debut and his first starring picture for First Artists Productions. Up until then, he was usually cast in lead roles and provided some input to directors on how a scene should be played. But never during his entire career had he sneaked behind the camera to supervise a feature-length film. He believed that he had the ability to direct as well as the talent to act, but had been afraid to utilize both in the same production. Now Hoffman would have the opportunity to do just that.

Straight Time was filmed at Folsom Prison in California and in downtown Los Angeles. Dustin was cast as an ex-convict who tries going straight after six years in prison, only to become ensnared in a life of crime. Also starring were Kathy Bates, Bonnie Bedelia, Gary Busey, Harry Dean Stanton, M. Emmet Walsh, and Clarence Williams III (of TV's "Mod Squad"). Stanley Beck and Tim Zinnemann were co-producing the film for Dustin under his own company, Sweet Wall Productions.

Dustin felt refreshed, his confidence restored, since, as director of *Straight Time*, he was in charge of his own destiny. He was also under the belief that *Straight Time* would be the film to smooth out any wounds incurred from *Marathon Man*. He realized that the public was usually forgiving, and so badly wanted *Straight Time* to succeed that he labored arduously for hours over reworking and rewriting the script, making sure it was meticulously detailed, leaving no room for human error.

Prior to location filming, Dustin visited the Los Angeles County jail to study the kind of atmosphere in which street offenders live. He was given the full treatment of inspection himself—just as if he were arrested—and went through the procedure of fingerprints and filling out department forms. Once he had a good idea of what a criminal goes through, someone suggested that the desk sergeant put Dustin's name up on the police computer board. The sergeant did just that for fun—but the result was less than hilarious: It showed that he had two unpaid traffic citations!

Hoffman paid his tickets, and went on to spend nearly eight months hanging out at prisons and county jails across the country, even managing to get smuggled in for several hours incognito at San Quentin prison. There he took some film footage illegally inside the prison and later mixed with ex-convicts in their trailer-park homes off the freeways of Los Angeles.

While Dustin was preparing for *Straight Time,* Anne was learning lines for her first screen role since *Papillon.* She was slated to star in Italian director Lina Wertmuller's new comedy featuring Giancarlo Giannini and Candice Bergen, called *It Never Rains But It Pours.* Anne, who had begun taking drama lessons earlier in the year, was to portray a friend of Bergen's in the film, which was released through Warner Bros. as Wertmuller's first film in English.

The situation was much different for Dustin as he was directing *Straight Time.* Finding the pressures in acting and directing the same production too great, Hoffman requested that his longtime friend, director Ulu

Grosbard, take his place as director of *Straight Time*. Grosbard was no stranger to Dustin, since he had directed the actor in *Who Is Harry Kellerman and Why Is He Saying Those Terrible Things About Me?* Hoffman gladly handed over the reigns to Grosbard when production resumed filming in Los Angeles on March 14. A spokesman for First Artists Productions said that no one forced Dustin to make the decision, but that he realized the movie was "just too demanding."

Around the same time, Hoffman became embroiled in rumors over his obsession with the film, causing him to spend nights in a hotel rather than with his family. The story soon went through several versions, including that he was separated from Anne. But Dustin later remarked that the arrangement was only during filming, with him returning home on the weekends to his family.

Straight Time remained a paramount personal concern, despite the vicious rumors about his marriage. Dustin became so concerned that he was often in the worst of moods, more on edge than ever, determined to avoid another failure. With Grosbard directing, production was stepped up and filming was completed in late September 1977.

Following a short hiatus, Dustin was already under way on his second film for First Artists, a film biography of Agatha Christie called *Agatha*. The film starred Dustin as an American journalist and Vanessa Redgrave in the title role, with filming commencing in London. The Christie family tried stopping production of the film but was unsuccessful. Dustin was originally given a part in *Agatha* the size of his first cameo appearance in *The Tiger Makes Out*. When First Artists understandably balked at the idea, Hoffman was cast in the second lead role. Afterward, he explained his reason for wanting the smaller role: "I'd play a part that was on the screen for ten minutes if I wanted to. I played second leads in *Midnight Cowboy, Papillon,* and *Agatha.* I just don't care." First Artists tried convincing him to start caring or they were going to refuse financing the film.

In order to rectify the situation, two new writers were brought in to "flesh out" the script and formulate a fuller character for Hoffman. Screenwriters Arthur Hopcraft and Murray Schisgal teamed with Kathleen Tynan, who had written a biography of Christie, to revamp the script so that production would continue as scheduled. Tynan remembers that Dustin was certainly satisfied with the original size of his role. "When he first saw it, he said it was one of the best things he had read in years. We formed the impression that he was quite happy to play the cameo role. Then the rewriting began." As Murray Schisgal added: "He [Hoffman] never quits. He can drive you up the wall sometimes, but Lord, he's got guts."

Rewriting the script was done in such a hurried fashion that some pages of dialogue were actually delivered at the last minute before a scene was filmed. The awkwardness of the procedure imposed an inexcusable threat to the performances of Hoffman and Redgrave, not to mention members of the supporting cast. Redgrave became so livid that she informed the director that she wouldn't act out any of her scenes unless her lines were written. Dustin, meanwhile, was steaming for a different reason. He just wished the production of *Agatha* had never started. "I literally got on my knees and begged them [First Artists] not to start the film. *Agatha* was every actor's nightmare. The script was literally being rewritten every day. It was a rainbow of green, yellow, and pink revision pages."

The order from the top brass to rewrite the script may have served as a warning sign. Hoffman became deeply concerned over his future at First Artists and the fate of his films while under contract to the company. In his opinion, *Agatha* was doomed to self-destruction without some creative control on his part, as his contract stated. And his first film for First Artists, *Straight Time*, was being readied for its March 16 theatrical release. Dustin wanted it postponed, giving him time to film a couple of new scenes at his own expense, but he never got that chance.

First Artists seized control of the picture, prompting Dustin to file a mutimillion-dollar legal suit against the parent company two weeks before the scheduled release. The legal action, filed at Los Angeles Superior Court on February 28, 1978, accused First Artists and its president, Phil Feldman, of seizing control of both *Straight Time* and *Agatha*, conspiring against Hoffman by taking over creative control of the projects. Dustin alleged that First Artists wouldn't grant him the right under his contract to cut the print of *Straight Time*, and that on February 4, the studio stopped filming of *Agatha* one scene short of completion. Hoffman was asking the court for an injunction against any editing, distribution, exhibition, or other use of *Straight Time* pending outcome of the trial.

Dustin outlined his grievances in a thirty-two-page complaint, in which he noted that his 1972 First Artists agreement granted him the exclusive right to produce two projects without pay, in exchange for creative and artistic control, including final editing. First Artists, he contended, was only able to take over control if costs of these productions skyrocketed. Hoffman did admit that *Straight Time* exceeded its original budget and that it took longer than first anticipated, but, he said, knowing the duration and cost of production, First Artists elected not to exercise any take-over right—even if they were legally able to do so.

After spelling out the facts, Hoffman was confident that he had built a sound legal case against First Artists for regaining control of *Straight Time.* The outlook for *Agatha,* however, was bleaker. The suit claimed that filming of the project was materially extended because of revisions in the script and by reason of contempt on the part of Redgrave, refusing to play various scenes unless they were written (accusations that screenwriter Kathleen Tynan has called untrue). In addition, Hoffman complained that First Artists repeatedly interfered on *Agatha* and demanded delivery of *Straight Time* by February 15, putting him "under great pressure." Dustin said also that he agreed to finish shooting *Agatha* before supervising the final editing of *Straight Time,* but that First Artists illegally ordered the final scene editing without his permission. In return of his damage suit, Hoffman was seeking over $2 million in lost salary on the films and over $66 million in damages resulting from breach of contract, with $3 million of that filed in exemplary damages against First Artists' president Phil Feldman and Jarvis Astaire, Dustin's business manager.

Court proceedings dragged on in the usual bureaucratic manner, however, and no attempt was made to stop distribution of *Straight Time,* which opened at the Bruin Theatre in Westwood, March 16, 1978. First Artists didn't have much regard for the film, so a press screening of the film wasn't held until the morning of its release. Usually that implies that the studio is hoping a late press screening will give the film an ample chance to generate good box office before any negative reviews are published.

Straight Time was Hoffman's fourth career catastrophe—with or without critical reviews. It was a hopeless, shamelessly exploitative film on the effect of the penal system. It had neither dimension nor character. Dustin produced a vivid account of an ex-convict's life, but the film's major drawbacks were a combination of a weakly constructed story, an inadequate supporting cast, and sloppy direction. Hoffman's performance is uneven as well. Strangely enough, he received no screen credit as a director or producer, only as a star. He probably wished he was able to have wiped his name off the film altogether, once critics were able to review it.

Straight Time casts Hoffman in the role of a luckless ex-con, Max Dembo, who is released from San Quentin prison after serving six years for an armed robbery charge. His freedom leads him to Los Angeles, where his parole officer (M. Emmet Walsh) pressures Dembo to make good. Through the efforts of his parole officer, Max sets up an interview with a metropolitan employment agency. An agency clerk (Theresa Russell) helps Dembo secure a job at a local canning plant, in order to appease his parole officer. The employment agency clerk eventually turns into Max's main love interest, sticking by him as long as he stays out of trouble.

But Max is unable to make his job last at the canning factory, getting canned, natch, and returning to what he knows best: crime. He hooks up with an old buddy (Gary Busey) and his nice, apprehensive wife (Kathy Bates), who are strung out on drugs. Busey and another accomplice (Harry Dean Stanton) end up as casualties after bungling a Beverly Hills jewelry heist. Dembo steers clear of any involvement in the burglary attempt, even though his eventual crimes lead him back to imprisonment. He does, however, avenge his pestiferous parole officer during his parole, in what becomes the film's sole humorous scene, handcuffing the officer to a freeway divider and pulling down his pants.

Straight Time provides no real insight into the penal system or criminals in general, following the typical cops-and-robbers mold. Perhaps the film might have succeeded if the characters, including Hoffman's, were not so one-dimensional and placid. The film not only lacks an alarming sense of drama, but a true understanding of the difficulty an ex-convict faces when he tries readjusting to society. Hoffman, in essence, surfaces as a prisoner not only in prison but in his own society, always a criminal, despite the different surroundings.

Dustin certainly appeared to be forever sweating in his role as Max Dembo. He seems rather uneasy, awkward, and unsure of his own screen characterizations of this ex-con, in the same way Ulu Grosbard seems unsure with his direction of the film. Theresa Russell is powerfully sexy in her role as Hoffman's girl friend, even though her performance suffers from unintelligible dialogue. Harry Dean Stanton, M. Emmet Walsh, and Gary Busey also try endlessly to win audiences in supplementary performances—but fail to impress.

Critics also threw the book at *Straight Time,* calling it far from Hoffman's best film and best performance. As *Los Angeles Times* critic Charles Champlin wrote in his review: "Hoffman's Max has less dimension than some of his earlier characterizations. You wish his fight had gone on a little longer." Perhaps harsher in his criticisms of Hoffman was *Time* critic Frank Rich: "Hoffman works hard and well to create a man who lives in a state of constant punishment. It's an admirable job, but one sadly wasted in a film that punishes the audience almost as much as it does the people on screen." Rich also blamed the film's vast problems on its "narrow spartan script." Unable to resist a humorous pun in reviewing the film, *Hollywood Reporter* critic Jeff Richardson added: "Warner Bros.' release owes the audience one thing: time off for good behavior. . . ."

By late July, final sentencing was the fact that *Straight Time* grossed only $4 million in box-office revenue, in attempting to recover the film's cost of $3.5 million (a film must gross nearly three times its budget to recoup all costs). First Artists, undoubtedly disgusted, pulled the film from theaters less than a year after its initial release. Ironically, the movie left theaters as quickly as it came during its eight-month playdate. Dustin doesn't like discussing the film, saying it "didn't realize anywhere near the potential it could have."

Ulu Grosbard, whom Hoffman brought in at the last minute to direct *Straight Time*, was reportedly not on speaking terms with Hoffman after the production was finished. Grosbard said that Dustin became too close to the work. "He had the project for five years, and he controlled it completely. By the time he called me, he had gone through four or five writers and six or seven drafts, and he had some of the best people in the field working for him. Dustin is a professional victim, and when you put yourself in that position, you can make preemptive strikes against everyone and feel righteous. I think he does care about quality, but that is not a license for his behavior."

In adding insult to injury, Los Angeles Superior Court Judge David A. Thomas rejected Hoffman's legal suit for seizing control of *Straight Time* and *Agatha*; his

former business manager, Jarvis Astaire, was countersu-
ing the actor for $3.5 million in damages; and his wife
of nearly ten years, Anne, was seeking a divorce from
the forty-one-year-old actor. Dustin couldn't have been
harder hit.

11

Breaking Up
Divorce, legal trouble with First Artists

Dustin had very little to be happy about. He was increasingly splitting his time between Hollywood and New York. Anne was divorcing him for what she has termed "mutual reasons." And his career was in need of some kind of boost.

Evidently, Hoffman's marriage began floundering when he was shooting *Straight Time*, in 1977. Anne's own career was beginning to take shape, which was partly responsible for the rift. On Anne's behalf, friends have said that Dustin was inconsistent in his emotions: After an enormous outpouring of charm and affection, he could turn icily distant. His roving eye was another reason for the breakup.

While divorce proceedings were under way, Anne remained in the Hoffman's Manhattan town house with Karina and Jennifer. Dustin bought a co-op apartment overlooking Central Park, which included an extra bedroom for the girls whenever they came to visit.

Life as a separated parent caused Dustin to return to

the singles scene. He was reportedly seen doing "the hustle" at New York's Studio 54 with Kate Jackson, who soon became his constant companion. He decided also to sprout a beard.

His life in a constant frenzy, Hoffman kept splitting his time between his plush three-bedroom apartment in Central Park and a house he was leasing in Westwood, California. Most of his time was being spent in Westwood, where he took daily bike rides to the Westwood Marquis Country Club for some leisurely exercise. Dustin frequently returned east to see his daughters. He put them both up at his apartment for overnight stays, even though their presence reminded him of his pending divorce.

Dustin began feeling sorry for his children because he felt it was unjust for them to suffer from his and Anne's mistakes. As he once explained, "You kid yourself if you think being separated does not have a traumatic effect on children. They are going to feel that it is somehow expected that they favor one parent over the other, and that causes conflict." Hoffman was also able to largely sympathize with his children's thinking on the possibility of living with him and Anne under the laws of joint custody. As he told an interviewer, "It doesn't sound like something I would want to experience if I were a child. I wouldn't want to experience it as an adult and I don't believe children are much different from adults."

Dustin has always been able to relate to children in general. He often describes himself as "crazy about kids." He just loves them—and they love him back. He can never get enough of them or their company. He isn't biased when it comes to loving just his daughters, though, as he loves everybody's children, including those of other friends. Hoffman's affinity for children stems from meeting Anne's first daughter, Karina. "I'd like to have as many children as possible. I first met Karina when she was three months old. With Jennifer, Anne and I went through natural childbirth exercises together. I was there for her birth and it was the most exciting thing I had ever experienced. Generally speaking, I don't think it's possible to give a child too much love. I try not to spoil mine, because I'm aware that there is a tendency to overcompensate when you're separated and don't see your children always," Dustin remarked recently.

Even though Dustin was hopeful that Anne and he could reconcile their differences, it never came to pass. Instead, he became accustomed to the life of a single parent, and the longer he was on his own, the more acceptable he found it. The single life gradually became the kind of challenge Hoffman liked exploring.

Dustin has never elaborated on what prompted Anne to leave him, though he once offered some insight in an interview. "The reasons are personal and complicated, as I'm sure they are for anyone else in this situation. Most separations come from the basic reason: Something is structurally wrong in the beginning. The territorial imperatives were wrong and that has come to make things very clouded." He went on, "But trying to be creative and spontaneous—that's the hardest part. That's one of the things, I'm sure, that prompts a lot of extracurricular affairs among people—what we call 'cheating.' What that comes from, I guess, is that the spontaneity breaks down."

Hoffman agreed also that sometimes people change objectives in their marriage as years pass, such as with his wife. Anne turned to acting on a full-time basis, even though it wasn't part of their original marital agreement. Needless to say, he feels that a two-career marriage must have something special going to make it succeed. "I'm in awe of the ones that work," Dustin confessed recently. The biggest drawback as a movie star, he feels, is the varying and hectic filming schedules. It oftentimes makes homelife close to miserable. "When I'm filming, my working day can start at five-thirty in the morning and not end before ten-thirty that night. And even when I get home, I still have to study the next day's script before crawling in bed. If you're married and have children and that schedule goes on for sixteen weeks, you are sacrificing your family," he says.

Hoffman is naturally envious of the days in Hollywood when actors were fortunate to film everything inside the perimeters of a studio. Some lived only twenty minutes away from the likes of Universal Pictures, Columbia Pictures, and Twentieth Century-Fox. Today, actors lead the lives of Gypsies—traipsing all over the countryside, working strange hours, and constantly feeling homesick. The glamour is there, but the methods of attaining it are "lousy," Dustin feels, especially if a family is involved. His own marital woes, in fact, started to occur while he was away filming *Straight Time*.

These were very emotional and complex times for Hoffman, still engaged in appealing his $68 million legal suit again First Artists for control of his films. Dustin has always been characterized as a very private person, who prefers keeping stories about his personal life out of the newspapers. He likewise avoids discussing particulars concerning his marriage. Whenever he conducts an interview, Hoffman always appears most happy to provide insights into his career and film achievements, since he feels that is what fans want to know the most. Moreover,

Dustin never tries glossing over the facts, unless he feels his answers might stain his public image or sound too degrading of others.

The emotional struggles eventually started to take their toll on the actor. He has admitted that the wave of confrontations—legal and personal—were enough to promote thoughts of quitting films altogether. "That's the trouble. I've said I would and I haven't done it. The day I don't say will probably be the day I'll do it," Dustin once confessed.

Hoffman felt he had just scratched the surface of his screen potential. He was yearning to find widely appealing roles that were as demanding as his previous film portrayals, but kept coming up empty-handed. Dustin was feeling that the first ten years of his career were a waste. His fans would undoubtedly be startled that he could feel that way because he had amassed in that same time a career full of admirable roles. Certainly, he has experienced his share of weaker films like any actor, but among them, Dustin has always been seen as a bright spot in these productions.

Hoffman has confessed that he considers his life of credits unmoving. "It's terrible feeling that your work hasn't been expressed anywhere near how it could be expressed. I keep feeling I haven't done anything yet. The need to be more of a painter seems to keep calling me. Until I satisfy that part of myself so that what I'm doing is not just an acting job but represents pretty much what I feel about the subject, I'll continue to feel I haven't done anything. *Midnight Cowboy* was more than eight years ago and I haven't even read a role like that since," Dustin said.

Certainly, the chances of uncovering a role as attractive as Ratso Rizzo sounded next to impossible, even though he eventually discovered one lead role that was appealing: as Ted Kramer in the screen version of Avery Corman's best-selling novel, *Kramer vs. Kramer*. The story was shaped around an outspoken father divorcing his wife, who decides she wants a career and thus leaves their five-year-old son with the father. The character of Kramer was more personal to Hoffman than any of his previous screen roles. The Kramer character offered Hoffman a chance to demonstrate the deep emotions he had for a character involved in a situation similar to his own.

Hoffman was originally sent a copy of the novel in 1977. He was considering the story as a potential film himself, rejecting it later for various reasons. "The novel seemed more contrived than I hoped it would be. I was equally unimpressed with the first script, written by director Robert Benton. They went through a lot of drafts and finally sent me another script. I got goose bumps from reading it and I said I would do it."

Producer Stanley Jaffe had no problems in buying film rights for the book—for an unspecified amount. But Benton and Jaffe had to show a great deal of patience in waiting for Dustin to accept the lead, since he turned them down *three* times before finally agreeing to their offer. His acceptance was made official when Jaffe offered him "full compensation" on the film—meaning artistic control.

Dustin has said that he fought for control in every phase of the film's production. "I told them, 'I want to be a collaborator. Otherwise, I'm going back to theater. I've had enough of this business.'" His reason, of course, was evident. First Artists had offered him artistic control for two films, reneging on the right at the last minute. If Dustin was to star in films again, artistic control was a necessity.

Jaffe saw no problems, and outlined in Hoffman's contract his controlling interests in the film. Besides having final say on editing, Dustin was free to improvise and request additional takes to alternative ideas he had in playing a scene. He was also given the opportunity to supervise the writing of the screenplay. The script was a collaborative effort on the part of Benton, Jaffe, and Hoffman, who spent over eight months reviewing the screenplay line for line. Benton admitted that Kramer's role was tailor-made for Dustin. Benton said, "I attempted to write the way Dustin talks, so that when he improvises, you wouldn't know the difference." Dustin's salary was also different: He was getting paid over $1 million and a share of percentages from the film's profits.

With the screenplay near completion, Dustin had a few matters to be ironed out before production began. The most crucial was selecting a qualified actress to play opposite Hoffman. Some film magazine columnists were reporting that Kate Jackson, Dustin's intimate companion, was given a firm offer to star as Hoffman's screen wife. But she turned down the offer because ABC wouldn't release her from her contract as star of TV's "Charlie's Angels." Consequently, at his suggestion, Meryl Streep was chosen to play Dustin's wife. Streep had made her fortune in such films as Alan Alda's controversial *The Seduction of Joe Tynan.*

The final task was finding a child actor to play Hoffman's five-year-old son. Dustin has said that Benton and Jaffe went along with him to various schools throughout the country, interviewing over three hundred candidates for the job. Hoffman became fond of a small seven-year-old who had the poise of Wallace Beery. His name was Justin Henry. Dustin wanted the blond, blue-eyed Justin, even though originally he flirted with the idea of using his daughter Jennifer. Dustin has admitted that he used his experience with Jennifer as a guide when acting out scenes with Justin. It was the kind of spirit that moved him and his peers.

To research the role of Kramer, Hoffman took an objective look at himself as a husband, a father, and a career person whose inner conflicts paralleled his screen character. In order to comprehend the character's motives, Dustin insisted on four weeks of rehearsal before actual filming began. As he told reporters on the set, "You can't rush quality. That's the key, but most people who make movies today aren't concerned with quality. All they're concerned about is making money."

Getting down his character—an obsession Hoffman has shown throughout his career—has been a distinguishable quality producers admire in the actor. "Dustin will spend as much time with a person as he's permitted, to get every last drop of blood until he has that down," producer Stanley Jaffe recalls. His costar Meryl Streep offered a different opinion of Hoffman. "He is a perfectionist about the craft and the structuring of the film, and his ego is subjugated to that." All of these known traits—perfectionism, producing quality films, understanding his characters—have been seen throughout Hoffman's colossal film career and have been almost single-handedly responsible for his success as an actor.

Kramer vs. Kramer started production on June 12, 1978, and was completed before Christmas, with filming taking place in New York. The film marked not only the directorial debut of Robert Benton, but also his first major screenplay adaptation. Location sequences were filmed in such settings as Camera Mart's Stage 54, which was originally the old Fox Studios. Dustin later became involved in supervising the editing and other postproduction work on *Kramer vs. Kramer*, before retreating to his Westwood home.

In seclusion, Dustin was able to reflect on other potential film and Broadway projects as the calendar pages soon turned to 1979. Of his projects, Hoffman was offered the lead role in Columbia Pictures' screen biography of musical composers George and Ira Gershwin, with Richard Dreyfuss as Ira and Hoffman as George. Besides film offers, he began reviewing scripts for a possible Broadway stage production and films he could direct, even though the emotional strain of his separation from Anne was still affecting him deeply.

Dustin, who fired himself as director of *Straight Time*, still had a burning desire to direct. As he once said, "I hope I don't act when I do direct. I'm in awe of the few who have done it successfully." Hoffman, remembering his disastrous debut as director of *Straight Time*, felt the pressure of holding down a trilogy of roles—actor, director, and producer—was the kind of burden he wouldn't accept, unless, of course, the situation was right.

12

Starting Over

Remarriage, *Kramer vs. Kramer*, the elusive Oscar

In the meantime, Dustin had high hopes for *Kramer vs. Kramer*, the sixteenth film of his career. It was a film, according to Hoffman, that was timely for him. Even though the role of Kramer was very like his own personality, he tried rebutting claims that Kramer was autobiographical. Instead, he has pointed out that some similarities exist between him and the character, but that essentially, he wasn't playing himself. "He [Kramer] touches on certain parts of myself that interest me," Dustin said in an interview during production. "But there's no such thing as yourself . . . I think it was Saul Steinberg [a Russian-born cartoonist] who said, 'I wake up every morning doing a different impersonation of myself.'" And that's exactly what Kramer was for Dustin.

The fact that *Kramer vs. Kramer* had been completed gave Hoffman enough time to concern himself with putting an end to his suit against First Artists. His second First Artists feature, *Agatha*, was being held from release because of his unwillingness to redub some inaudible tracks of dialogue for the film. First Artists had its prayers answered when Dustin unexpectedly stopped at a London studio, during a trip overseas, to reloop the necessary dialogue. Newspaper accounts were citing Hoffman's cooperation as the initial step to First Artists' announcing the screen release of *Agatha*. Sure enough, that following afternoon, First Artists made it official that *Agatha* was being prepared for theatrical distribution and that a special private screening was being arranged for critics in New York and Los Angeles.

First Artists realized that Hoffman wasn't going to let *Agatha* go out to theaters flawed. "I had always hoped he would loop the dialogue," remarked Michael Apted, the film's director. "Secretly, I thought that Dustin wouldn't allow the film to go out without trying to make it the best film possible." As Dennis Feldman, a First Artists executive, added: "We didn't want anyone to see the picture without it having his best performance."

Consequently, *Agatha* made its world premiere on February 9, 1979, at New York's Cinema I Theater. The film was a biographical docudrama about one of the world's foremost literary figures, Agatha Christie. Screenplay credit went to Kathleen Tynan, who wrote the novel of the same title, and Arthur Hopcraft. Johnny Mandel, an Oscar-winning composer, wrote and conducted the score. *Agatha* was also the second and last Hoffman production under his Sweet Wall Productions film company outlet in association with First Artists. Unlike his First Artists release of *Straight Time*, his second go-round was much more successful and critics were strongly favorable. Filmgoers also turned out in droves to catch the film.

Set in 1926, *Agatha* is fashioned after the actual disappearance of famed mystery writer, Agatha Christie (Vanessa Redgrave). Agatha is distraught over news that her war-hero husband (played by Timothy Dalton) wants a divorce so he can marry his earthy secretary. She stages a disappearance, which causes an international stir.

While hordes of Britons hunt for the missing author, she reappears at a resort hotel on the Yorkshire coast where she has registered under the name of her husband's mistress. A young American journalist, Wally Stanton (Dustin Hoffman), locates Agatha and quickly falls in love with her (Hoffman is dwarfed by Redgrave, who towers over him by nearly three inches). Love and romance permeate the remaining plot line, with Hoffman and Redgrave's romantic interludes taking up almost all of what remains of the story.

Hoffman's performance is bold, and bolsters the touchingly comic coupling of him with Vanessa Redgrave. He is clean-shaven and dapperly attired throughout the film. At first, his role seems almost incidental to the story, until, of course, he and Redgrave meet. He is in control of his character and of every scene. Redgrave, meanwhile, delights audiences with her gawky, sorrowing performance of Agatha Christie, literally wrapping herself around Hoffman when they kiss. Director Michael Apted efficiently captures the atmosphere of the period, thanks in large part to the shimmering photography of cameraman Vittorio Storaro (who also photographed *Apocalypse Now, Last Tango in Paris,* and *1900*).

In the eyes of most critics, *Agatha* was the surprise film treat of the year, handsomely produced, not quite a mystery but a love story, and rather a borderline biography and drama. Though the screenplay was suspect at certain points in the film, *Agatha* manages to rise to the occasion as a result of Hoffman and Redgrave's resourcefulness. Some reviews agreed that the film was a captivating period piece that utilized a similar decor to that in *Murder on the Orient Express* and *Death on the Nile*, two Agatha Christie stories adapted as movies.

The New York Times critic Vincent Canby expressed his own satisfaction with the film when he said: "Mr. Hoffman lands a good deal of humor in a role he appears to have made up—his mannerisms anyway—though you never for a moment believe he could fall in love with such a desperate character [Redgrave]." Canby stated also that *Agatha* may have been a movie breakthrough since "for the first time a leading man has been dwarfed by a leading lady without damage to either reputation." Without a doubt, Redgrave stole the show.

Even Richard Schickel, a veteran critic for *Time* magazine, didn't waver in his support of the film. He wrote that *Agatha* was "a very nice movie: quietly, slyly witty; confident enough of its virtues to take its sweet time in telling its story, and marked by two endearing performances." *Newsweek* critic David Ansen also jumped on the bandwagon, saying, "*Agatha* is a delight. Using short, enigmatic scenes that keep the viewer perpetually off-balance, director Michael Apted carries a wonderfully atmospheric Christie world, full of fog, suspicion and slightly worn elegances."

First Artists and Hoffman were hoping that Ansen meant the kind of magic that good box office was built on. His predictions were remarkably accurate in that respect, since the film did create some kind of historic magic at the box office. During the first six months, *Agatha* grossed about $4 million, which was what *Straight Time* had grossed in about a year. Even though Hoffman's original version of his role was never conveyed, according to him anyway, the film managed to stand up on all counts.

What Hoffman had hoped to prove as the male antagonist opposite Redgrave was "a reverse image of Streisand and Redford in *The Way We Were.*" As one writer commented on Dustin's philosophy, "The only effective contrast is between Redgrave's and Hoffman's heights."

Though Hoffman's vision of a Redford-Streisand reversal was never fully realized, the film was a modest success and concluded Hoffman's activities at First Artists. He had lived up to his two-picture contract, but because of legal hassles he had no desire to continue his association with the company.

With a short break from film-making and pressing speaking engagements, Dustin made periodic stops in New York and overseas to Cannes, France. While in Manhattan, Hoffman got together with an old friend and while overseas made a new one. One afternoon, Dustin was seen having lunch at the Russian Tea Room in New York with his former film partner, Jon Voight. They sat recalling the good times in *Midnight Cowboy* and discussing Voight's success in his latest movie, *Coming Home.* At the time, Voight had also finished filming *The Champ* for MGM, playing the role Wallace Beery originated in 1931. Hoffman expressed to Voight his desire to return to Broadway, provided that Jon would join him.

Then, in the late summer of 1979, Dustin flew to Cannes where he was seen with a girl who became his constant companion for a short time: Barra Gable, a beauty from a neighboring town. But, according to a friend, Gable wasn't necessarily his new lady. "Dustin's a constant flirt," his friend remarked, who suggested that may have been one reason for his marital woes with Anne. Indeed, Dustin's relationship with the tall, seductive blonde didn't last very long. Instead, Hoffman found greener pastures when he returned to America, though he kept in contact with Gable. Dustin only enhanced his reputation as a flirt during these months of separation from Anne, when he told one New York reporter, "I've always found women very sexy when they're pregnant, unless, of course, they're smoking. That gives me the chills." He also hinted at the time to some friends that he wanted to start another family—and soon. Married or unmarried, Hoffman was unable to cope with living by himself. As he later admitted, "It's nice to have someone there when you need them, which is many times during the day. As long as there's someone in the house somewhere, it's very comforting."

Hoffman also ticked off what attracts him to women. He likes someone who's sexy and beautiful but whose exterior is secondary to the inner self. Dustin says, "I've been most attracted to women who were working behind counters—salesgirls, waitresses, working girls—rather than rich women who go shopping every day." He also enjoys a woman whom he regards as an equal—someone who challenges him intellectually, nurtures his creativity, and keeps him on his feet emotionally.

Even though Dustin likes to fantasize about his role as a "great womanizer," he's pointed out that it's no secret. He is a romantic person who, when struck with the right mood, can be a flirt. In the wake of his confession, though, he has made it clear that he is basically a one-woman man.

Around the time of his return to America that October, Hoffman also started preparing to promote the Thanksgiving release of *Kramer vs. Kramer*. In numerous interviews, Dustin discussed how challenging the film was and what rewards he gained from working with Streep and young Justin Henry. He said that Streep and he had some "bad fights," but that they were always fights over the same thing—the construction or playing of a scene. Hoffman has admitted, however, that he felt intimidated to best Streep in every scene, since her performance was always so demanding (in a restaurant scene, Dustin got so angry over Streep upstaging him that he topped the actress by shattering a wineglass against a wall).

Dustin likewise worked closely with Justin Henry, the youngster who was playing his son in the film. "He [Hoffman] kept Justin from being just another cute kid," director Robert Benton says. "When it came to do a scene, Dustin would sit and talk alone with Justin, get him to be tougher or madder or sadder." The two also developed a personal father-and-son relationship on the set, Benton added. Benton does concede that "someone as obsessed as Dustin creates a lot of tension and puts a tremendous burden on the people he's working with," adding that he would be hesitant in the future to work with the actor again.

Up close and personal, Dustin had been described as solemn and bawdy, charming and outrageous, an articulate man "who sometimes stumbles over words and jabs his fingers redundantly into the air to help make his point." Hoffman argues that he isn't as difficult as people make him out to be. As he once reasoned: "If that means I don't go along with other people's opinions, then I've been difficult ever since I started. I got kicked out of acting class when I was twenty years old because I screamed at the teacher when she started talking to me in the middle of a scene. I had a big fight with Lee Strasberg in my first class with him. I got fired from Off-Broadway and I quit shows. I have never felt unbrave. If a picture is a success, they'll say, 'If that's what they call difficult, I'll take it anytime.'"

Perhaps Hoffman is right. When *Kramer vs. Kramer* opened to theaters nationwide in November 1979, critics and fans kept reiterating that the ninety-five-minute movie entertained, made them cry, and made them laugh. Maybe the popularity of Hoffman's Ted Kramer character stemmed from changing attitudes in America. Kramer appears to be the strong male role model audiences can identify with in the 1980s, much the same as filmgoers did with Clint Eastwood's Dirty Harry in the 1970s.

Kramer vs. Kramer is the kind of story that certainly relates to the get-divorced feelings of couples today. The film opens with Ted Kramer's vault up the ladder of success because he's landed his advertising agency's most valued new account. He is so caught up with his career that he pays less attention to what is happening at home with his wife, Joanna (Meryl Streep), and his son, Billy (Justin Henry).

When Kramer returns home to inform Joanna that he has won one of the best advertising accounts in New York, Joanna informs him that she's leaving him, never to return. He first thinks she's joking, asking her to explain her reasons and what is bothering her. Joanna's answer is more cut-and-dried than he is able to fathom: She walks out of the apartment door, baggage in hand, then unfeelingly tells Ted she doesn't love him anymore. The crushing blow of reality penetrates his deep emotions, and he accuses his neighbor Margaret (Jane Alexander), a divorced parent, of advising Joanna to make such a decision (later he apologizes and they become the closest of friends). He remarks to Joanna before her departure, "You just loused up one of the five best days of my life," only seeing how it affects his career and not his personal life—until later.

The story shows the life of a single parent—the struggle of adjusting to raising a child alone. Some amusing scenes result, however: Dustin trying to make french toast (always telling Billy, "I'm having a good time, aren't you having a good time?" as if to convince himself), burning the toast and blaming it on Joanna for walking out on him. In another scene, Dustin and Justin are seen shopping at a local supermarket, with Justin replacing any items Hoffman selects because Mommy used her own brands. Another amusing scene is when Ted wakes up after spending a night with his agency's legal attorney. The woman attorney excuses herself to the bathroom, meeting a sleepy-eyed Billy in the hallway, trying to cover up her stark-naked body (Justin stops her to ask what her favorite meal is).

Filmgoers see also the emotional, traumatic side of a separation in the manner in which it affects not only the parent but the child. Hoffman clears out his apartment of any belongings that remind him of Joanna (for example, picture frames, scrapbooks), wiping the slate clean in order to start anew. On occasion, Billy bursts into tears in the caring arms of Hoffman, wondering whether Joanna will ever return. His single parenthood is also exploited when Billy injures himself while playing on some monkey bars. His accident requires emergency stitches at a local hospital, where a panicky Hoffman oversees the operation.

The emotional damage increases when Joanna returns to New York after months of therapy in California, finding work in advertising herself, and requests legal custody of Billy. The emotional trauma of a legal court battle ensues, with the attorneys of both parties playing dirty in order to win the case. Following the onslaught of judicial proceedings, Joanna emerges victorious in gaining custody of Billy, with a depressed, irate Hoffman learning the news from his attorney. Billy doesn't want to leave Ted, however, staying with him when Joanna decides Billy is better off with his father.

Hoffman endears himself to the audience in a performance that comes close to his best. He convinces audiences that the suffering of a separation usually coincides with a great deal of personal risk. He comes across as powerful, demanding, loving, sincere, emotional, in fact, many of the same emotions evident in his other performances but not to the same high degree of realism.

Streep also rises to the occasion, the perfect counterpart for Hoffman as his screen wife, Joanna. She is equally demonstrative and believable under the standards of divorced women today. She is also the right kind of vibrant personality to complement Dustin, since she is as much of a scene-stealer as he is. Justin Henry likewise convinces in his performance as the self-centered five-year-old caught between the love for his father and mother. Robert Benton's debut as a director is exceedingly deliberate in making what could have been a contrived story breeze along. The film also contains superbly acted performances from its supporting cast of Jane Alexander, Howard Duff, and George Coe. Cameraman Nestor Almendros's stunning photography has lots of punch and variety.

Kramer vs. Kramer was not only a filmgoers' favorite but also that of film critics everywhere. As *Daily Variety* noted: "Hoffman gives his best performance in years. Streep is haunting in what is essentially a minor role. . . . In a picture about men leaving women, and women leaving men, no one has grappled with the issue in such forthright and honest fashion as *Kramer*." Roger Angell of

The New Yorker magazine said: "*Kramer vs. Kramer* is so good that you want it to be a masterpiece instead of a tearjerker and a nearly perfect miniature." And *The New York Times* critic Vincent Canby was calling the character of Ted Kramer "one of the two or three best roles of his [Hoffman's] career."

Kramer vs. Kramer was the movie that surely kept filmgoers buzzing for months. It packed theaters almost every night, even on weeknights following the Christmas season, enabling Dustin to climb back up to the top of cinematic superstardom. The film not only grossed over $75 million in less than six months, but topped over $100 million after its release overseas.

Because of *Kramer vs. Kramer,* the kind of cinematic recognition that often escaped Hoffman during his career seemed close at hand. Hoffman was saluted in Dallas, Texas, as part of a series retrospective on his career, featuring films the actor personally selected: *Midnight Cowboy,* *Little Big Man,* and *Lenny.* He even made some appearances at universities and colleges, discussing the film after a special screening to standing-room-only audiences. In Williamsburg, Pennsylvania, the American Film Institute scheduled its first special film event, a special screening of *Kramer vs. Kramer.*

Even the Golden Globe Awards nominated him best actor in a motion-picture drama, besting Jack Lemmon, Al Pacino, Jon Voight, and James Wood. But Dustin explained later that evening that he didn't like such competitions, that he preferred the film itself to endure because of its performance. As he told an applauding, star-filled audience at the Beverly Hilton, scene of the thirty-seventh annual Golden Globe presentation, "People will forget who won this year in a very short time. But that work, which is done, which is created, will live in the hearts of all people that see it, whether it wins or it doesn't win."

While Hoffman did not turn back his award, afterward he handed his Golden Globe to Kramer producer Stanley Jaffe. In addressing his fellow nominees, Dustin asserted that "awards make more sense when they're given for a life achievement to a man like Henry Fonda and particularly to a man like Jack Lemmon (who gave one of the greatest performances of his life in *The China Syndrome*)." Hoffman did find some time to add humor to his acceptance speech, first saying, "I want to thank divorce." But Dustin's putdown of the industry's proliferation of awards was typical of his attitude.

Although Dustin may not have fully appreciated the significance of these awards, critics and judges of other film award societies continued to nominate him. The twenty-two-member Los Angeles Film Critics Association voted Robert Benton's *Kramer vs. Kramer* as the decisive winner among the best picture category, Benton as best director, and Hoffman as best actor of the year. Meryl Streep was also chosen best supporting actress. The Los Angeles critics' awards presentation was followed by the granddaddy of them all: the fifty-second annual Academy Awards ceremonies.

Dustin had been to the Oscar sweepstakes before, losing every time. Yet, according to Las Vegas oddsmakers, *Kramer vs. Kramer* was the clear favorite to capture the best picture honors, with Hoffman singled out as the leading candidate for best actor over Peter Sellers *(Being There)*, Al Pacino *(. . . And Justice for All)*, Roy Scheider *(All That Jazz)*, and Jack Lemmon *(The China Syndrome)*. Robert Benton was nominated for best director, while Meryl Streep was the favorite for best supporting actress. Her competition was Jane Alexander (also of *Kramer vs. Kramer*), Candice Bergen *(Starting Over)*, Mariel Hemingway *(Manhattan)*, and Barbara Barrie *(Breaking Away)*. The festive ceremonies were also to be highlighted by the presentation of a life achievement award to actor Sir Alec Guinness, with Dustin serving as presenter and moderator of the ceremony.

On April 14, 1980, tension began to build, with Hoffman preparing for his speech on Alec Guinness while hundreds of other nominees took their seats early at Hollywood's Dorothy Chandler Pavilion. Before the decisive category winners were announced, Dustin stepped up to the microphone early in the show to the resounding cheers of the throng to introduce Sir Alec Guinness. Perhaps, the overwhelming applause was to serve as a signal to Dustin that he would soon return to the stage for another reason. Hoffman gave a very eloquent speech, calling Guinness "what I think all actors should strive to be. I know of no other actors in the story of film who touched this man's work and it's a great tribute to introduce him to you." Guinness came out of the wings, emerging to a standing ovation, looking dapper with thatches of gray hair lining his baldpate. He was congenial in thanking Dustin for his kind introduction, exiting from the stage after delivering his own dignified acceptance speech.

Later that evening, Dustin was the winner as best actor of the year, feeling enormously proud of the achievement, despite his negative attitude toward such awards. His peers finally honored him with an Oscar. Now, with some of the best performances behind him, it was a screen character so close to his own that had captured the coveted honor. Hoffman was also proud that a film as dramatically touching as *Kramer vs. Kramer* had stolen so many Academy Award honors. Meryl Streep took the award as best supporting actress, while Robert Benton won in the category of best director. *Kramer vs. Kramer* also garnered best picture of the year honors, with these awards representing the tops among all categories.

Dustin was also given the news that he had topped a recent popularity poll published by *People* magazine. The question of the poll was, "Who is your favorite actor?" It was no contest: Hoffman beat out everybody by a wide margin, topping such stars as Paul Newman, Burt Reynolds, Robert Redford, and Sylvester Stallone, who rated last.

Certainly, the combined winnings of an Academy Award and major popularity poll enabled Hoffman to have more bargaining power in negotiating with studios. In fact, these awards quickly paid off when Columbia Pictures announced the signing of Hoffman to a three-picture deal. His first starring production under the pact is *Tootsie*, which is scheduled for release in late 1982. Columbia signed the actor to a $4.5 million contract to star in the film, which Sydney Pollack is directing. *Tootsie* revolves around plots similar to that done in *Charley's Aunt*, starring Jack Benny, and *Some Like It Hot*, with Jack Lemmon. Hoffman will portray a starving New York actor who decks out in drag in order to win the role of a nurse on a TV soap opera. The screenplay was written by Murray Schisgal, Hoffman's longtime associate. Hoffman is also developing a number of other film projects for Columbia including *Laughing War*, based on the best-selling novel; and a baseball comedy of *Long Gone*, with Dustin as manager of a 1940s minor-league team. Dustin was also being considered for the lead in the film version of *Gorky Park*, but he turned it down.

During his two-year absence from the screen, Dustin has seen a number of changes in his life. His divorce from Anne was made final, and during the summer of 1980 he married a twenty-five-year-old law school graduate, Lisa Gottsegen. Dustin and Lisa had first met when she was a teen-ager visiting her grandparents, who live near Dustin's parents in Los Angeles. As a friend of Hoffman's said, "They are very much in love." In 1981, *People* magazine again named Dustin as the top actor in its poll of readers' favorite actors, this time topping Robert Redford, Clint Eastwood, and Burt Reynolds. He also beat out Robert DeNiro, who won best actor for *Raging Bull*, and John Travolta, who was last. Dustin appeared also for the second year in a row as a presenter at the annual Academy Awards show.

Of equal importance to Dustin Hoffman, the actor, is Dustin Hoffman, the man. As Meryl Streep says of him, "He's the kind of person you'd wish were your father. He is very entertaining and he knows how to address a child not as a child but not as an adult either—in their language." Hoffman has been described as a practical jokester at times, lively, a lover of children, and the life of the party. He is cautious about his commitments in the film world, since his number-one priority before taking on any project is "the story. It's the key. It's no secret that a very good story told in a mediocre way works, while even a very good job done on something that lacks a story, doesn't."

Hoffman is at ease with friends and others who surround him. Even when he goes out for a walk, the actor enjoys working out mannerisms and dialects—sometimes in public. Once while out shopping with a friend in Beverly Hills, he was on the receiving end of a phone call inside a quaint boutique, imitating the salesman's French

accent over the phone. A few minutes later, he supposedly also started blowing bubbles out of saliva, to the
utter astonishment of customers around him.

Another time, while inside the Beverly Hills' Nei-
man-Marcus store, Dustin noticed a tall neat-looking
black man in one of the departments wearing a yellow
jogging suit and matching headband, trying on an expen-
sive jacket. The scene tickled Dustin so much that he remarked, "Now that's specific. That's a visual specific.
You won't see that anywhere but Beverly Hills."

Dustin's other familiar trait is his constant use of
quotes from famous poets, writers, and artists of our
time. During conversations with one writer, Hoffman began sprinkling his answers with quotes from Buster Keaton, e.e. cummings, and Norman Mailer. He explained
what causes him to use these passages: "I do it habitually, I can trace it back to grammar school. I would imi-
tate teachers, and in order to do that, you would have to
observe them. For some reason, I had this tremendous
voyeuristic aspect." Friends even admit that he never actually reads books for quotes but instead skims through
them for some good lines.

Hoffman is also a very energetic person. On a typical
nonfilming day, he gets up at 5:30 or 6 A.M. and goes
through the ritual of preparing a noncaffeinated, barley-
based wake-up drink called Pero. Then, he reads the
newspaper, jumps rope for twenty minutes to rock music, and tries reading a book or play a day. That same
afternoon, Dustin might meet with a small group of his
New York friends: Murray Schisgal, Joseph Heller, and
David Goodman. When in Los Angeles, where he still
leases a house, Dustin will spend time in the company of
his friends screenwriter Robert Towne and director Hal
Ashby. He admits that despite the fact that he enjoys his

friends' company, he doesn't make it a habit. As the day wears down, Hoffman then makes it a point to watch at least one movie a day to study techniques in acting and directing, before retiring for the night by midnight.

Dustin considers himself a good cook and he doesn't smoke, drink, or gamble. His only vice is swearing, of which he says, "I use bad language because I like to shock people." In real life, he tries ignoring the labels people have put on him, such as "movie star," "a matinee idol," and "sex symbol." He considers it a compliment that the public views him in that manner, but he prefers to remain like just "one of the boys."

In spite of the wide variety of comments that have been circulated over his reputation as a difficult actor, Hoffman tries conveying one feeling as an actor in his work. "All I know is I try to be as personal as I can in my work, by being personal, to be able to bring to it a truth in what I observe and what I feel," he says.

In the meantime, while he continues to stun film audiences with new roles, Dustin will always keep looking. "I think it was Einstein who said, 'Never make a living doing what you love.' For me, it's trying to hit the perfect ball. If I go down tomorrow, I'll have gone down trying to hit the perfect ball."

With that remark, Hoffman can't miss—he's destined to go down in the history of film as "Dustin Hoffman: Hollywood's Antihero."

Filmography

The Tiger Makes Out (Columbia Pictures, 1967)
Producer: George Justin
Director: Arthur Hiller
Screenplay: Murray Schisgal
Based on his play, *The Tiger*.
Director of Photography: Arthur J. Ornitz, A.S.C.
Film Editor: Robert C. Jones
Music: Milton (Shorty) Rogers
Cast: Eli Wallach (Ben), Anne Jackson (Gloria), Bob Dishy (Jerry), John Hawkins (Leo), Ruth White (Mrs. Kelly), Roland Wood (Mr. Kelly), Rae Allen (Beverly), Sudie Bond (Miss Lane), David Burns (Mr. Ratner), Jack Fletcher (Pawnbroker), Bibi Osterwald (Mrs. Ratner), Charles Nelson Reilly (Registrar), Frances Sternhagen (Lady on bus), Elizabeth Wilson (Receptionist), Kim August (Tony Songbird), Alice Beardsley (Neighbor), Mariclare Costello (Rose), David Doyle (Housing clerk), Dustin Hoffman (Hap), Michele Kesten (Waitress), and James Luisi (Pete Copolla).
Running Time: 94 minutes

The Graduate (Embassy Pictures, 1967)
Producer: Lawrence Turman
Director: Mike Nichols
Screenplay: Calder Willingham, Buck Henry
Based on the novel by Charles Webb.
Director of Photography: Robert Surtees, A.S.C.
Film Editor: Sam O'Steen
Music: Dave Grusin
Songs by Paul Simon (sung by Simon and Garfunkle)
Cast: Anne Bancroft (Mrs. Robinson), Dustin Hoffman (Benjamin Braddock), Katharine Ross (Elaine Robinson), William Daniels (Mr. Braddock), Elizabeth Wilson (Mrs. Braddock), Buck Henry (Room Clerk), and Brian Avery (Carl Smith).
Running Time: 105 minutes

Midnight Cowboy (United Artists, 1969)
Producer: Jerome Hellman
Director: John Schlesinger
Screenplay: Waldo Salt
Based on the novel by James Leo Herlihy.
Director of Photography: Adam Holender, A.S.C.
Film Editor: Hugh A. Robertson
Cast: Dustin Hoffman (Ratso Rizzo), Jon Voight (Joe Buck), Sylvia Miles (Cass), John McGiver (Mr. O'Daniel), Brenda Vaccaro (Shirley), and Bernard Hughes (Towny).
Running Time: 113 minutes

John and Mary (Twentieth Century-Fox, 1969)
Producer: Ben Kadish
Director: Peter Yates
Screenplay: John Mortimer
Based on the novel by Mervyn Jones.
Director of Photography: Gayne Rescher, A.S.C.
Film Editor: Frank P. Keller
Music: Quincy Jones
Cast: Dustin Hoffman (John), Mia Farrow (Mary), Michael Tolan (James), Sunny Griffin (Ruth), Stanley Beck (Ernest),

Tyne Daly (Hilary), Alix Elias (Jane), Julie Garfield (Fran), Marvin Letcherman (Dean), Marian Mercer (Mags Eliot), Susan Taylor (Minnie), Olympia Duhahis (John's mother), Carl Parker (Tennis player), Richard Clarke (Charlie), Cleavon Little (Film director), Marilyn Chris (Film director's wife), Alexander Cort (Imaginary film director), and Kristoffer Tabon (Boy Scout).
Running Time: 92 minutes

Madigan's Millions (American International Pictures, 1969)
Producer: Sidney Pink
Director: Stanley Prager
Screenplay: James Henaghan, J. L. Bayonas
Director of Photography: Manolo Rojas, A.S.C.
Film Editor: Antonio Ramirez
Music: G. Cregory Sigura
Cast: Dustin Hoffman (Jason Fister), Cesar Romero (Mike Madigan), and Elsa Martinelli (Vicki Shaw).
Running Time: 76 minutes

Little Big Man (National General Pictures, 1970)
Producer: Stuart Millar
Director: Arthur Penn
Screenplay: Calder Willingham
Based on the novel by Thomas Berger.
Director of Photography: Harry Stradling, Jr., A.S.C.
Film Editor: Dede Allen
Music: John Hammond
Cast: Dustin Hoffman (Jack Crabb), Faye Dunaway (Mrs. Pendrake), Martin Balsam (Merriweather), Richard Mulligan (Gen. Custer), Chief Dan George (Old Lodge Skins), Jeff Corey (Wild Bill Hickock), Amy Eccles (Sunshine), Kelly Jean Peters (Olga), Carol Androsky (Caroline), Robert Little Star (Little Horse), Cal Bellini (Younger Bear), Thayer Davis (The Reverend Mr. Pendrake), Ray Dimas (Young Jack Crabb), and Alan Howard (Adolescent Jack Crabb).
Running Time: 147 minutes

Straw Dogs (Cinerama, 1971)
Producer: David Melnick
Director: Sam Peckinpah
Screenplay: David Zelag Goodin, Sam Peckinpah
Based on the novel by Gordon M. Williams.
Director of Photography: John Coquillon, A.S.C.
Film Editor: Paul Davies
Music: Jerry Fielding
Cast: Dustin Hoffman (David), Susan George (Amy), Peter
Vaughan (Tom Hedden), T.P. McKenna (Major Scott), Del
Henney (Venner), Ken Hutchinson (Scutt), Colin Welland
(Rev. Hood), Jim Norton (Cawsey), Sally Thornsett (Janice),
Donald Webster (Riddaway), Len Jones (Bobby Hedden),
Michael Mandel (Bertie Hedden), Peter Arne (John Niles),
Robert Keegan (Harry Ware), Jane Brown (Mrs. Hedden),
Chloe Franks (Emma Hedden), and Cherina Man (Mrs. Hood).
Running Time: 118 minutes

*Who Is Harry Kellerman and Why Is He Saying Those Terrible
Things About Me?* (National General Pictures, 1971)
Producer: Herb Gardner, Ulu Grosbard
Director: Ulu Grosbard
Screenplay: Herb Gardner
Director of Photography: Victor J. Kemper, A.S.C.
Film Editor: Barry Malkin
Music: Shel Silverstein
Cast: Dustin Hoffman (Georgie Saloway), Barbara Harris (Alli-
son Densmore), David Burns (Leon Saloway, Georgie's father),
Jack Warden (Dr. Solomon F. Moses), Gabriel Dell (Sidney
Gill), Betty Walker (Margot Saloway), Rose Gregorio (Gloria
Saloway), Dom DeLuise (Irwin Matsy), Regina Babi (Ruthie
Tresh), David Galef (Leonard Saloway), and Ed Zimmerman
(Peter Halloran).
Running Time: 108 minutes

Papillon (Allied Artists, 1973)
Producer: Robert Dorfmann, Franklin J. Schaffner

Executive Producer: Ted Richmond
Director: Franklin J. Schaffner
Screenplay: Dalton Trumbo, Lorenzo Semple, Jr.
Based on the novel by Henri Charriere.
Director of Photography: Fred Koenekamp, A.S.C.
Film Editor: Robert Swink
Music: Jerry Goldsmith
Cast: Steve McQueen (Papillon), Dustin Hoffman (Louis Dega), Victor Jory (Indian Chief), Don Gordon (Julot), Anthony Zerbe (Toussaint), Robert Deman (Maturette), Woodrow Parfrey (Clusiot), Bill Mumy (Lariot), George Coulouris (Dr. Chutal), Ratna Assan (Zoraima), William Smithers (Warden Barrot), Val Avery (Pascal), Gregory Sierra (Antonio), Victor Tayback (Sergeant), Mills Watson (Guard), Ron Soble (Santini), Barbara Morrison (Mother Superior), Don Hanmer (Butterfly trader), E.J. Andre (Old Con), Richard Angarola (Commandant), Jack Denbo (Classification officer), Len Lesser (Guard), John Quade (Masked Breton), Fred Sadoff (Deputy Warden), Allen Jaffe (Turnkey), and Liam Dunn (Old trustee).
Running Time: 150 minutes

Alfredo, Alfredo (Paramount Pictures, 1973)
Producer: (uncredited)
Director: Pietro Germi
Screenplay: Leo Benvenuti, Pietro de Bernardi, Tullio Pinelli, Pietro Germi
Director of Photography: Alice Parolin
Film Editor: Sergio Nontanari
Cast: Dustin Hoffman (Alfredo), Stefanià Sandrelli (Mariarosa), Carla Gravina (Carolina), Clara Colosino (Carolina's mother), Daniele Patella (Carolina's father), Danika LaLoggia (Mariarosa's mother), Saro Urzi (Mariarosa's father), Louigi Baghetti (Alfredo's father), and Duilio Del Prete (Orste).
Running Time: 97 minutes

Lenny (United Artists, 1974)
Producer: Marvin Worth

Executive Producer: David V. Picker
Director: Bob Fosse
Screenplay: Julian Barry
Based on Julian Barry's play.
Director of Photography: Bruce Surtees, A.S.C.
Film Editor: Alan Helm
Cast: Dustin Hoffman (Lenny Bruce), Valerie Perrine (Honey Bruce), Jan Miner (Sally Marr), Stanley Beck (Artie Silver), Gary Morton (Sherman Hart), Rashel Novikoff (Aunt Mema), Lee Sandman, Martin Begley, Monroe Myers, Bruce McLaughlin (Judges), Mike Murphy, Richard Friedman, Bob Collins (District Attorneys), Mark Harris, Ted Sorrell, Clarence Thomas (Defense Attorneys), Allison Goldstein, Bridghid Glass, Susan Malnick (Kitty Bruce as a child), John DiSanti (Time reporter), and Jack Nagle (Rev. Mooney).
Running Time: 111 minutes

All the President's Men (Warner Bros., 1976)
Producer: Walter Coblenz
Director: Alan J. Pakula
Screenplay: William Goldman
Based on the book by Carl Bernstein and Bob Woodward.
Director of Photography: Gordon Willis, A.S.C.
Film Editor: Robert L. Wolfe
Music: David Shire
Cast: Dustin Hoffman (Carl Bernstein), Robert Redford (Bob Woodward), Jack Warden (Harry Rosenfeld), Martin Balsam (Howard Simons), Hal Holbrook (Deep Throat), Jason Robards (Ben Bradlee), Jane Alexander (Bookkeeper), Meredith Baxter (Debbie Sloan), Ned Beaty (Dardis), Stephen Collins (Hugh Sloan, Jr.), Penny Fuller (Sally), John McMartin (Foreign editor), Robert Walden (Donald Segretti), and Frank Wills (Himself).
Running Time: 136 minutes

Marathon Man (Paramount Pictures, 1976)
Producer: Robert Evans, Sidney Beckerman

Director: John Schlesinger
Screenplay: William Goldman
Based on his novel.
Director of Photography: Conrad Hall, A.S.C.
Film Editor: Jim Clark
Music: Michael Small
Cast: Dustin Hoffman (Babe Levy), Laurence Olivier (Szell), Roy Scheider (Doc Levy), William Devane (Janeway), Marthe Keller (Elsa), Fritz Weaver (Professor), Richard Bright (Karl), Marc Lawrence (Erhard), Allen Joseph (Mr. Levy), Tito Goya (Melendez), Ben Dova (Szell's brother), Lou Gilbert (Rosenbaum), Jacques Marin (LeClerc), James Wing Woo (Chen), Nicole Deslauriers (Nicole), and Lotta Andor-Palfi (Old Lady in Street).
Running Time: 125 minutes

Straight Time (Warner Bros., 1978)
Producers: Stanley Beck, Tim Zinnemann
Director: Ulu Grosbard (uncredited for his directorial work, Dustin Hoffman)
Screenplay: Alvin Sargent, Edward Bunker, Jeffrey Boam
Director of Photography: Owen Roizman
Film Editors: Sam O'Steen, Randy Roberts
Cast: Dustin Hoffman (Max Dembo), Theresa Russell (Jenny Mercer), Harry Dean Stanton (Jerry Schue), Gary Busey (Willy Darren), M. Emmet Walsh (Earl Frank), Sandy Baron (Manny), Kathy Bates (Selma Darren), Edward Bunker (Mickey), Stuart Barton (Salesman #1), Barry Cahill (Salesman #2), Corey Rand (Carlos), James Ray (Manager), Rita Taggert (Carol Schue), and Frank Ryan (Cafe owner).
Running Time: 114 minutes

Agatha (Warner Bros., 1979)
Producer: Jarvis Astaire, Gavrik Losey
Director: Michael Apted
Screenplay: Kathleen Tynan, Arthur Hopcraft
Based on the novel by Kathleen Tynan.

Director of Photography: Victorio Storaro
Film Editor: Jim Clark
Music: Johnny Mandel
Cast: Dustin Hoffman (Wally Stanton), Vanessa Redgrave (Agatha Christie), Timothy Dalton (Archie Christie), Helen Morse (Evelyn), Cilia Gregory (Nancy Neale), Tony Britton (William Collins), Timothy West (Kenward), Allan Badel (Lord Brackenbury), Paul Brooke (John Foster), Carolyn Pickles (Charlotte Fisher), Robert Longden (Pettelson), Donald Nithsdale (Uncle Jones), Yvonne Gilian (Mrs. Braithwaite), David Hargreaves (Sergeant Jarvis), Sandra Voe (Therapist), Barry Hart (Superintendent MacDonald), Tim Seely (Capt. Rankin), and Jill Summers (Nancy's aunt).
Running Time: 98 minutes

Kramer Vs. Kramer (Columbia Pictures, 1979)
Producer: Stanley R. Jaffe
Director: Robert Benton
Screenplay: Robert Benton
Based on the novel by Avery Corman.
Director of Photography: Nestor Almendros, A.S.C.
Film Editor: Jerry Greenberg
Music: Henry Purcell
Cast: Dustin Hoffman (Ted Kramer), Meryl Streep (Joanna Kramer), Jane Alexander (Margaret Phelps), Justin Henry (Billy Kramer), Howard Duff (John Shaunessy), George Coe (Jim O'Connor), JoBeth Williams (Phyllis Bernard), and Bill Moor (Gressen).
Running Time: 105 minutes

Bibliography

Almendros, Nestor. "The Invisible Cinematography of *Kramer vs. Kramer.*" *Millimeter*, March 1980, pp. 37–44.
Ball, Aimee Lee. "Dustin Hoffman vs. Dustin Hoffman." *Redbook*, vol. 154, no. 4 (February 1980), pp. 33, 158–161.
Chapman, D. "Graduate Turns Bum." *Look*, September 16, 1968, pp. 66–72.
Clarke, Gerald. "A Father Finds His Son." *Time*, vol. 114, no. 23 (December 3, 1979), pp. 78–79.
deDubovay, Diane. "Dustin Hoffman: Man in Conflict." *Ladies' Home Journal*, February 1980, pp. 82, 168–172.
Galluzo, Tony. "Dustin Hoffman Hums a Few Bars of Deadpan Humor." *Motion Picture Herald*, January 17, 1968, p. 8.
Groller, Ingrid. "Dustin Hoffman Talks About His Daughters, His Separation, His Career." *Parents*, December 1979, pp. 38–42.
Gussow, M. "Dustin Hoffman: An Interview." *McCalls*, September 1968, pp. 143–144.
McKinney, Doug. *Sam Peckinpah*. Boston, Mass.: Twayne Publishers, 1975.
Mellen, Joan. *Big Bad Wolves: Masculinity in the American Film*. New York: Pantheon Books, 1977.

Morella, Joe, and Epstein, Edward Z. *Rebels: The Rebel Hero Films.* Secaucus, N.J.: Citadel Press, 1971.

Probst, Leonard. *Off Camera.* Briarcliff Manor, N.Y.: Stein & Day, 1975.

Shipman, David. *The Great Movie Stars.* New York: A&W Visual Library, 1972.

Spada, James. *The Films of Robert Redford.* Secaucus, N.J.: Citadel Press, 1977.

Tretick, Stanley. "Off the Screen." *People,* May 3, 1976, pp. 52, 55–57.

Willis, John. *Theatre World.* New York: Crown Publishers, vols. 1966, 1968, 1968, 1975.

Winfrey, Carey. "Cinema: The Moonchild and the Fifth Beatle." *Time,* vol. 93, no. 6 (February 7, 1969), pp. 52–54.

Zeitlin, D. "Movies." *Life,* November 24, 1967, pp. 111–112.

Index

167